Words large as apples

Words large as apples

Teaching poetry 11–18

Mike Hayhoe
and
Stephen Parker

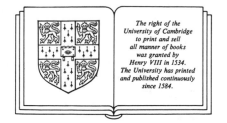

The right of the
University of Cambridge
to print and sell
all manner of books
was granted by
Henry VIII in 1534.
The University has printed
and published continuously
since 1584.

CAMBRIDGE UNIVERSITY PRESS

Cambridge
New York   New Rochelle   Melbourne   Sydney

Published by the Press Syndicate of the University of Cambridge
The Pitt Building, Trumpington Street, Cambridge CB2 1RP
32 East 57th Street, New York, NY 10022, USA
10 Stamford Road, Oakleigh, Melbourne 3166, Australia

First published 1988

Printed in Great Britain at the University Press, Cambridge

British Library cataloguing in publication data
Hayhoe, Mike
    Words large as apples: teaching poetry 11–18
1. Poetry, Application – For schools
I. Title   II. Parker, Stephen
809.1'01

Library of Congress cataloging-in-publication data
Hayhoe, Mike
    Words large as apples: teaching poetry 11–18
Mike Hayhoe and Stephen Parker
1. Poetry – Study and teaching (Secondary)
I. Parker, Stephen (Stephen James)   II. Title
PN1101.H39 1988
808.1'07'1241 – dc19   88-10292 CIP

ISBN 0 521 33114 5 hard covers
ISBN 0 521 33731 3 paperback

CE

Contents

The following abbreviations are used to refer to three popular and useful anthologies:

RB   *The Rattlebag*   edited by Seamus Heaney and Ted Hughes (Faber and Faber, 1982).

T   *Telescope*   edited by Eric Williams (Edward Arnold, 1974).

TWF   *Touched With Fire*   edited by Jack Hydes (Cambridge University Press, 1985).

1

Why 'teach' poetry?

'Please, Miss, a poem's a set of words with a riddle in the middle!' That was shouted out by a pupil after his student-teacher, a shrewdly patient woman, had given her class of twelve-year-olds the task of rummaging through poetry books virtually every lesson for two weeks, with the instruction, 'Tell me what a poem is'. There was a moment's silence, a sense of satisfaction. They had 'solved' the puzzle of what a poem is – that it is, ultimately, strong enough and rich enough to resist any neat solution.

Therein lies the joy of poetry for many people. Therein can lie many of our problems in the classroom. You can see the positive attitude towards the elusiveness of a poem in D.H. Lawrence's rather heady celebration:

> Poetry is a matter of words. Poetry is a stringing together of words in a ripple and jingle and run of colours. Poetry is an interplay of images. Poetry is the irridescent suggestion of an idea. Poetry is all these things and still it is something else.

It is exciting to have pupils who enjoy that sense of a poem still being 'something else' which will not allow itself to be fixed or solved. Such pupils lighten the day – theirs and yours. But others see poetry differently. Take Sam Weller's father in *Pickwick Papers*, for instance, as Sam prepares to write a Valentine for him:

> ''Tain't in poetry, is it?' interposed his father.
> 'No, no,' replied Sam.
> 'Werry glad to hear it,' said Mr. Weller. 'Poetry's unnat'ral.'

It is only mildly consoling to find that pupils who consider poetry 'boring' or 'stupid' are inheritors of an attitude which began long before any of us went to school!

In a sense, Sam Weller's father was right. Poetry does seem unnatural, or at least odd, to many people. Compare it with three features of a prose tale. Firstly, most people will read a short story or a novel for enjoyment, since these literary forms feel familiar. We tell stories and listen to one another's gossip; we watch stories on television and at the cinema; we read them in newspapers. In other words, we encounter stories in many different media and we absorb a complex set of skills in order to understand them and respond to them. It all feels very ordinary and natural. Secondly, stories often tend to be a bit like life because of their length. We can live with them over several days, or weeks, or even years, in the case of a successful television 'soap'. We feel easy with them as we grow alongside them. Thirdly, stories often build in a lot of guidance on how to read them. A story-teller such as Enid Blyton was particularly strong at building in plenty of clues to interpretation. '"I DO think it's *mean!*" said George fiercely.' Its capital 'DO', italicised 'mean', exclamation mark and adverb certainly provide a young reader with plenty of clues on how to generate a 'George' in his or her mind. Think also of how we use gesture and all sorts of variation in voice when we tell a story; of how a film uses such devices as music and close-up to give us clues – and so on.

Compare these three features – familiarity, duration and interpretive clues – with what happens in the world of poetry. Firstly, most pupils do not see poetry as 'familiar', particularly since they tend to associate it with only one medium, print. Secondly, most poetry is unusually terse, presenting its case far more succinctly than most stories do. It is often condensed and elliptical, relying more on what it suggests than on what it states. Thirdly, it tends to be sparing with the clues it offers for interpretation. In other words, it 'asks' rather than 'gives': it makes demands for great attention, interpretation and conjecture on the part of the reader. It expects a readiness to speculate, to call upon all one's experience of life, to venture, to take risks. Pupils encounter stories every day of their lives; poetry may feel very unfamiliar. Pupils who are not used to the demands a poem makes (or who are unaware of the nature of its rewards) are very likely to be daunted.

And yet. That view of poetry may be true some of the time, but it is not always so. Poetry is not necessarily some arcane mystery created by an esoteric 'them' to be passed on through initiatory rites to novices. It can be argued that poetry has roots which are certainly as natural and 'ordinary' as those for a story. If poetry is about emotion, as Wordsworth said it was, then it is worth noting just how often we do use language to express and reflect on emotions, moods and responses. Some of our feelings may be expressed in narrative; quite often they are not. Deeply emotional experiences often leave us inarticulate; we even say that we are 'lost for words'. The genius of any poet is to make raids on the inarticulate, to try to see and to say, so that we can formulate our own version. A teenager in love; a child with a first puppy; having to cope with the shock of being the victim of an injustice; the long term gnawing of resentment; the exhilaration of a motorbike ride; the grief of a bad examination result – the seedbed of the emotions is with us at all times.

Poetry is 'ordinary' in another sense – its means of expression. It grows from the everyday habit of using our communal possession, language. Moreover, most people enjoy playing with language, just as they enjoy other inventive games; they enjoy using their skill of making the extraordinary out of the ordinary. For instance, think of children's (and others') delight in jokes and outrageous puns. As individuals, even babies will play with repeating a sound over and over again for the sheer joy of its achievement, its sound and the physical act of making it. As social beings, people enjoy the repetition of rhythm and rhyme in such forms as football chants, skipping rhymes, television jingles and many songs. It is not always recognised that even tabloid newspapers echo poetry as they use the Anglo-Saxon poetic device in their headlines of what might be called 'front rhyme' (or alliteration) as in the emotive BABY BORN EARLY FOR DYING DAD.

Linguists call unusual uses of language 'marked', meaning that they are noticeable. In a sense, all of us find situations in which we use language in some special way. It can be said that a football chant is 'marked'. The wish to say something special in a special way can involve a smaller group: the sad *In Memoriam* columns in a local newspaper show how often people turn to some features of poetry in order to control and intensify what they have to say, to give it some shape and memorability. Christmas and birthday cards often contain language which has been made special through imagery and rhyme. Some people will protest that none of these represents genuine poetry; but the important point is that all of them harness a natural wish to give some form to expressions of emotion, so that they will last and have power. Finally, there are the efforts that most people make at some time to create poetry – or to re-create it by trying to inhabit and explore the words offered by someone else.

It is worth stopping briefly to see where the words *poem, poetry* and *poet* come from: the Greek 'to make; to fashion'. In Anglo-Saxon times, a poet was called a 'scop', a work akin to our word 'shape'. Poets make. Poets shape. They make their shapes out of words. The shapes they make may appeal to our visual sense. They may appeal to our aural sense by using rhyme and rhythm. They may appeal to our sense of physical involvement as we actually say them and maybe move to them. At their best, they appeal to us through our senses, our emotions, and our intellect. They say for us what we also would like to say, helping us to ask what living is, and to make meaning out of our lives. Like any other well-crafted objects, they exist to be experienced and are admired for what they do and what they are. We like a 'good' poem for what it enables us to do in thinking and feeling; we also appreciate it for its own form as well.

Much of a school's curriculum deals with what is often called 'the real world' of facts and objective study, often in codified and managed forms. It is necessary that pupils encounter such areas as mathematics and the sciences. It is also sensible that they meet 'the real world' in terms of practical subjects, careers advice and work experience programmes. But there is a third 'real

world', of exploring the nature of existence and what significance it may
have. That is where the arts have a part to play, including those based upon
our most ordinary and yet central skill, language – and poetry is one of these.
Poetry exists in the world beyond the school and therefore is part of our
proper business inside it. It is an aspect of the curriculum which provides the
opportunity and obligation to feel as well as think, to recognise the talent of
an individual as well as the society in which he or she lived or lives. It is a
means of exploring beyond the logical and the immediately, practically
'relevant'. That notion of 'beyond' is important. Poetry is not a fanciful,
trivial activity which can be lost from the curriculum. We are arguing that,
with its linguistic challenge and its invitation to explore and celebrate every
aspect of existence by going beyond objectivity, poetry undertakes a major
role in helping many people to grow. Given the proper climate, poetry gives
shape to and celebrates existence; it also challenges and questions. We have
tried to set out approaches which will not 'teach' poetry but provide
opportunities for its educative powers to operate.

Wordsworth regretted a world which he thought had become too obsessed
with the practical and with the material, so that it had lost its sense of
wonder. There is a great sadness in his lines:

> The world is too much with us; late and soon,
>   Getting and spending, we lay waste our powers:
> We have given our hearts away, a sordid boon!

Some might share that sadness. Others might prefer a more positive
perspective, seeing poetry as central to many of us in balancing our vision of
the world. Perhaps it is one of the subjects that Aristotle had in mind with his
challenging words:

> There is such a thing as a subject in which we must educate our
> sons, not because it is useful, but because it is fine and worthy of
> free men.

Substituting 'children' for 'sons', and 'people' for 'men', this book aims to
help in this task of ensuring that poetry is everyone's experience, everyone's
property.

This book sets out to describe approaches which practising teachers find
helpful in encouraging pupils to venture into poetry, and in encouraging
them to bring with them their own equipment of emotion, thought and
language, and of personal and communal experience. Many of these
approaches depart from the apparently detached attitude and cool elegance
of the adult critical essay or review; some do not. Our main aim has been to
show something of the range of approaches which all of us can call upon
when we ask of our pupils these two things: firstly, to be moved by the poem
– maybe shifted emotionally, maybe in attitude; secondly, to be interested in
how the poem and the reader, partly in collaboration with one another and

partly in a state of challenge, bring about these emotional and intellectual shifts. In other words, this book aims to promote a reflective response which is akin to D.H. Lawrence's definition – forgive his sexism – when he wrote as the first line of a poem, 'Thought is a man in his wholeness wholly attending'.

There is no justification for time spent with poetry to be static, with pupils receiving 'the right answers' about poems and regurgitating them as neat essays, replete with half-understood technical terms. Where does active thought find a place in such an approach? Where is there room for an exploration of poem and reader? Where is the potential for collaborative or private active learning, or the chance to venture? This book argues the case for active approaches which encourage genuine, exploratory, and pro-visional responses – a readiness to visit a poem and revisit it from a variety of angles rather than 'solve' it and leave it.

Several chapters look specifically at how working through the senses – whether visually, or through sound or through drama – can help to focus such open thoughtfulness. The discussion of writing centres on the increasing awareness that pupils grow in their response to poetry by experiencing the dilemmas, challenges and choices of being poets themselves. One chapter looks at how younger pupils can experiment with poetic form; another looks at how experimentation can be used with seniors to increase their sense of a poem as an artifact. Many of the activities that we suggest involve group work, following poetry's long tradition of being an occasion for communal celebration and exploration. This seems to us one of the main arguments for poetry's place in the curriculum. At the same time, it is worth remembering that poetry can also be very personal. Time and space and teacherly patience should be available for a pupil's privacy and reticence, for 'silence', when poet and poem and reader get on with their proper, mutual business. Such provision is not usual in the school timetable, but it is essential that we provide the conditions for this active silence. Schools often talk of helping to develop the individual. We can help to create a climate in which individuals can develop themselves.

The theorists who have informed our thinking about poetry exist in our examples of good practice rather than in summaries of what they have to say. Seeing their insights in action seems the best tribute to them and to the teachers who have adopted their ideas – or from whose ideas the theories arose in the first place. We hope that you will find much here that you are already practising and much that you can try out, adapt and adopt in the venture of providing a climate for poetry in and beyond the classroom.

2

Getting and sharing information

At the beginning of any school year pupils will usually come to us as unknown quantities; but they will, of course, have a wealth of experiences, attitudes and beliefs about the world, about schooling and about poetry. Sometimes these will be negative, and the older children get, the more likely that is to be the case with regard to poetry. It is often the worst possible approach to present a new class with direct questions about these experiences and attitudes. They may see this as confrontational, and if they groan at the very word 'poetry', where do you go next? Although it is highly desirable to know what pupils think about poetry, and what they have met and liked before, discussion needs to be handled very sensitively in the first instance.

Poem cluster workshops

A less intrusive way to begin is with a practical assignment such as a poem cluster workshop which will indirectly reveal pupils' attitudes and experiences, at the same time (one hopes) giving them an experience of poetry which they will enjoy and learn from. It will call on them to examine a group of poems in the light of their own experience.

First choose a topic which is in very common experience, on which they are likely to have opinions. Take for example the topic of 'Cats'. Ask the class first of all to think of a cat; not just any cat, but a particular cat which they can see in their mind's eye; closing their eyes might help, if the class does not think this too childish. Then ask them to write down, as quickly and spontaneously as possible, phrases which describe the cat; its colour, shape, movement, and perhaps contrasts of mood – playful, hunting, hungry. Then in pairs or small groups they discuss what they have written. Only after they have confidently established their own vision do they encounter poetry. It must be more than one poem, hence the notion of a 'cluster' around the same topic but from different points of view: some negative, some positive and all seeing the topic from a different perspective. The poems chosen should represent a wide range of possible attitudes towards cats – and there is no shortage of divergent views on that topic.

Pupils are asked to find phrases and expressions in one or more of the poems which are like their own cat vision. In asking pupils to select phrases, we are really asking them to select perceptions, to see things through the poet's eyes. The notion of 'perceptions' is too abstract though, and to speak of 'phrases' is preferable since it is a more concrete concept than images or perceptions. The process of choosing phrases creates a lot of discussion, as well as a close consideration of the poems, but without the exhaustive analysis of a comprehension exercise which might be off-putting. Pupils can disagree in safety with some of the poems selected, even with all of them, but only on the basis of having established an alternative perception. If pupils say they 'do not like the poems', then the response is to say, 'Well, we must write our own; let's hear how you saw your cats.' So creative writing can be integrated with this approach.

Essentially, this approach asks pupils to:
- focus first on the real-life experience and write down snapshots of their perception.
- discuss and compare experiences with others.
- encounter a range of poetry which relates to their own experience.
- contrast the poet's experience with their own.

Through this process pupils gain confidence in their own judgment: their own experience is absorbed into their learning, they are allowed genuinely to criticise poetry, in that they accept some phrases and they reject others, and they encounter a lot of poetry without having to express orthodox views. Although this technique is described here for use in a first encounter with a class, it is in effect a basic teaching technique which will continue throughout schooling. (See Appendix 1b for additional guidelines.)

Personal journal

Such classroom assignments as the above call for a relatively public response, and hence are not completely to the taste of all pupils, or suitable for all occasions. Alongside such a public response may be the writing of a personal journal or log, in part written voluntarily in free moments and at home, though perhaps the basic minimum might be specified for the occasional homework. It need not be marked in as much as it need not be graded and assessed, though the teacher could usefully respond to it as a sympathetic reader.

The subject of the journal will be a personal response to poetry, and the very fact that the journal exists will motivate pupils to look for poetry beyond the brief encounters in English classes. Pupils might write about poetry and their response to it in pop songs, advertising, and snippets such as headlines in newspapers. Journal writing makes teachers aware of the need to make poetry anthologies available in classroom and library, and to talk about TV and radio poetry programmes – before the event to encourage pupils to watch or listen, and after to encourage the sharing of responses.

The essential idea of journal writing is that it should be spontaneous; correct spelling and syntax are of less importance than a genuine personal response to whatever strikes the pupil about a poem, about the experience behind the poem, or the experience of the lesson. As for the role of the teacher there are two possible approaches, which will significantly affect the kind of writing produced:

1. Where the journal is semi-private, and the teacher collects them in very infrequently. The journal is therefore a kind of diary and is treated as confidential by the teacher who is a privileged reader.
2. Where the journal is written only on one side of the page, the facing page being left blank for the response of someone else – either a writing partner (a trusted pupil-friend in the class) and/or the teacher. The response is therefore made very frequently, and is a kind of dialogue between the writer and trusted readers.

Conferencing

Workshop lessons such as the poem cluster give the teacher time and opportunity to talk and interact with pupils, either one to one or in small groups. Through the journal individual pupils can write mainly for themselves and partly to the teacher: but it is much more valuable if the dialogue of the journal is complemented by individual tutorials. The teacher, then, should meet individual pupils on a regular basis to talk freely about literature; not as an examiner but as an interested and informed adult, offering not only advice but also a ready ear.

Such conversations need not be solely with the teacher. If pupils work in twos to produce a 'paired journal', the partners will want to talk over their responses. Even where the writing is not paired, pupils can be paired at intervals for brief discussions, reading extracts from their journals aloud to each other for comment.

Feedback

In between the relative formality of class lessons and the relative privacy of tutorials, there lies the area of informal interaction between teacher and students in a variety of groupings, which is a natural feature of a classroom with a positive poetry climate. As trust builds up over a period of time, individual students should begin to feel less sensitive about talking to the whole class about their thoughts and feelings, having had the chance to work these out in the journal, and talk them over with a trusted listener.

This kind of interaction with the whole class may take place spontaneously, but a forum for it can also be built into the overall programme. Tell students some time in advance that a lesson will be set aside for them to talk about the poetry they have encountered over a period of time. Let them set an agenda, with volunteers agreeing to start discussion about issues which they themselves nominate. If there is a list of topics and poem titles are put up on the bulletin board, those who wish can re-read, prepare themselves and plan what they might say. Often students are seemingly inarticulate in class debate because they have not had enough time to think out in advance their attitudes to the subjects under discussion.

Bulletin board

Once the feeling arises that there is a continuing poetry programme, there will be increasing reason for information to be posted on a bulletin board, for example:

- dates of tutorials with students in the class.
- publicity for coming TV and Radio programmes about poetry.
- publicity for local arts events.
- copies of students' writing, perhaps with artwork added and made into poetry posters.
- attractive pictures illustrating a published poem.
- a thematic display, a composite of students' and published poetry with pictures and artwork.

Open bookshelf

Although the school library is likely to have a poetry section, that is a relatively remote source of material. Classes of children never finish their work at the same moment and we always need activities for those who complete tasks ahead of the rest. If there is a poetry collection available on a shelf in the classroom, then browsing is always possible. New books, old books, anthologies or single author collections – variety is the key to the interest such an Aladdin's cave should hold. Anthologies for a younger age range than that of the class concerned may give the browser confidence in seeing the familiar, of re-visiting best-loved poems.

The same use can be made of cassette tapes of poetry readings, stored on the shelf and with a cassette player and headphones or listening centre available nearby. BBC Schools Broadcasting produces a range of poetry programmes, or programmes which are an anthology of poetry and prose around a theme. They are usually bright, lively and entertaining, particularly those with a commentary, and all are suitable for students to listen to either solo, with headphones on, or in small groups. It is an ideal activity for the early-finisher; someone who has finished a task before the rest, to a good standard, and so can be given something else to do which is enjoyable and worthwhile. A constant danger in the classroom is to punish the early-finisher by setting additional work which is neither interesting nor enjoyable. The hidden curriculum can so easily suggest that humdrum conformity and slowing to the pace of the slowest is what teachers want of students.

Assignment sheets might be housed in this collection, related to particular collections or individual poems. This would require a more formal response, though it need not be limited to comprehension exercises and 'fill-in-the-blanks' worksheets. For instance students might act as research assistants for future lessons by finding poem clusters, or search for poems for other classes, or for ballads which involve betrayal ... and so on.

If the magazine of the Schools Poetry Association is also put on the shelf on open access, students will see that poetry is not just a backwater of eclectic academic knowledge. Magazine browsing appeals strongly to teenagers. Psychology suggests that they are in a stage where group attitudes are of prime importance, and values of the teenage sub-culture are often carried by magazines. If we can add poetry magazines to that category we can perhaps extend that sub-culture.

Outside links

Many city and county libraries have specialist children's librarians who spend a great deal of time in keeping up with current publications in order to make the appropriate purchases and recommendations for readers. They can also help schools to keep up with current publications, which is otherwise a difficult task, involving the reading of reviews and publishers' catalogues, and sending for specimen copies – and who likes sending the rejects back? It can be a very hit and miss process. But to have an active link with librarians can only be of benefit to schools. If you know the library staff, you will get to hear of recent acquisitions and you may be able to arrange for individual students to go to the library for a particular homework assignment. The library is also likely to know of local and national groups concerned to promote poetry writing or study or performance.

Visiting writers schemes

In this respect the Regional Arts Associations play a key role. Their 'Visiting Writers' scheme sponsors visits to schools by poets and teachers who talk about their work or run activity-based workshops. Meeting a 'real poet' has universally proved to be a great motivator for children's own writing and in stimulating a positive attitude towards poetry. A catalogue of available writers usually lists the kind of topics and teaching approaches which they prefer, so it should be possible to match your context with the right poet. However it is always best if you can to talk to colleagues in other schools about their experiences of visiting writers, and to take recommendations.

Teacher networks

'Networks' for the exchange of information between local schools probably exist in all parts of the country through such associations as the National

Association of Teachers of English. Poetry will come into the brief of a local NATE group at least occasionally, and if not in recent memory, perhaps the committee will accept requests from the membership for particular topics. In some areas there may also be more informal teachers' groups set up to promote poetry. The local teachers' centre would be the best place to make enquiries if you want to find such a group – or want to set one up: it takes initiative but the teachers' centre warden may well want to help by offering a mailing service, perhaps a roof over the group's head when it meets, or publicity for its activities as well as for recruitment.

Eisteddfods

Interest for teachers and students can be given an occasional boost with a major event such as an eisteddfod, or some form of poetry reading event; or a festival of a more varied kind based around writers and exhibitions of their work, which brings together pupils to enjoy new workshop ideas, and teachers to share techniques and gain fresh stimulus. Working together to organise such a festival is one of the most powerful and constructive ways for a group of teachers in an area to establish real contacts between themselves for professional interest and development. Before and after the big event such contacts will be less pressured, but continued contact will be a potentially invaluable source of teaching techniques, materials, and stimuli for the classroom.

3

Creating a positive climate

In discussing how to create a positive climate for encounters with poetry, perhaps the most obvious comment to make is that the phrase 'positive climate' is far too glib a term for a very complicated state of affairs. There is a lot you can do to bring that positive climate about, but there is little point in blaming yourself if you do not always succeed.

The teacher's role

What can be done? The first thing, perhaps, is to be honest about your relationship with poetry. That means letting the pupils become aware of how their teacher thinks and feels, without dominating their own responses. For example, a certain poet or poem may have little effect on you – just as certain foods or pictures or music do not appeal. That does not mean that you indulge in the perennial adolescent response of 'it's boring' or 'it's stupid', but it can be an opportunity at some point to say, 'This poem and I are not getting on. How about you? Any idea why?' Similarly, if a poem puzzles, no adult should be afraid of owning up. 'Hmm, I don't get that bit at all,' is an acknowledgement of your thought processes which some pupils (the 'you're-paid-to-teach-us' brigade) may find disconcerting. It can also be turned around, to provide an occasion for pupils to help sort out your puzzlement or for them to admit their puzzlement, without loss of self-esteem. At best, such moments provide an occasion for co-operative rummaging, for communal tentativeness – the positive attitude towards exploration which is what we are trying to foster.

Finally, there is the more conventionally positive honesty, of enthusing about poetry you do like. Bearing witness, showing commitment, is an essential component of teaching success. One teacher is amiably accepted for coming into lessons and saying, 'I know we said we were going to do some work on *Macbeth* this afternoon, but just listen to this for a couple of minutes,' and he reads a brief poem or piece of poetic writing which has particularly moved him, sometimes to sadness, often to laughter. He moves quickly to the lesson's official business, leaving his reading to fade, perhaps, in some minds and, perhaps, to echo in others. Another teacher every now and then declares her tastes: 'I'd like to share with you some poems that mean a lot to me. I hope you'll like them or come to like them, but please be careful if you don't. Don't trample on them.' And she runs a couple of sessions in which she shares poems which are important to her, for instance with fifteen-year-old pupils, looking at some poems by Yeats.

This chapter starts with the teacher because in many classes, when it comes to poetry, the pupils insist on focusing on the teacher. To them, stories are much more obvious and familiar. 'Poetry' is frequently regarded as much more divorced from the large world of narrative. It is often seen as deliberately getting rid of 'story', of using language which is deliberately 'special', of being something posh, silly and deliberately obtuse. These partial misconceptions lead at least some pupils to resign from the challenge of the poem before them and to assume that they can rely on you to sort the poem out for them.

It is important that such dependence on the teacher is not allowed to grow, for it does nobody any good. Of course, there will be occasions when you can help young readers to respond more fully and richly than they would have on their own, but poets do not write in order to have an adult 'expert' constantly mediate between their poems and their readers. If we regularly accept the role of expert which some pupils would impose on us, we allow them to duck addressing what it is in themselves which the poem has encountered. If we constantly impose ourselves in the role of expert, we get in the way of pupils developing their own expertise. It is important, therefore, to provide opportunities again and again for pupils to share both in providing the poetry and in setting the agenda for the approaches to be used. The second of these aims of everyone contributing to a growing response to poetry, is the main topic of the rest of this book. This chapter is more concerned with some of the ways in which teachers and students can be colleagues in providing the poetry in the first place and, in so doing, can produce a mutually supportive and exploratory climate.

Clearly these two aims cannot be neatly separated; nor should we try. Ideally, we are trying to make poems as 'ordinary' as stories – fictions which we feel it natural to encounter and to share. The Bradford Book Flood experiment shed some light on this (see Joan Ingham, *Books and Reading Development*, Heinemann Education, 1981). A number of schools were flooded with books. But where there was no personal supportive context, the books were seen as an invasion and reading actually declined. Opportunity was seen as confrontation, providing confusion and proof of incompetence on the part of the reader. In other schools in the experiment, staff and students constantly chatted about what they were reading, exchanging news and views – and reading prospered. That constant and growing sense of mutuality is what we have to aim for through a 'Poems Around the Place' policy.

Poems around the place: sounds

One of the obvious benefits of technology has been the easy retention and dissemination of sounds, for example with the tape-recorder and through broadcasting. That, in turn, has promoted the restoration of poetry as sound and allowed it to be heard across years and cultures and, sometimes, by millions of people at one time. The experience of poetry which is communicable through this medium can be startling, as, for instance, when senior students hear the stoic, austere voice of T.S. Eliot reading his *Four Quartets* poems and struggling with his almost unsayable thoughts. It can also be something as startling as a pop record. The point is that there are many recordings available which employ words in a special way, to operate beyond any literal meaning – and use the sound of them to create at least part of their effect. An Elizabethan sonneteer or a nineteenth-century Lancastrian folk-singer used to play with the sounds of words and with musical setting just as a Caribbean poet or a rock lyricist may do today. Every age has enjoyed the sound of poetry; ours is no exception. It is important that we and our students should seek the excellent in our own time, as well as valuing the excellent from the past. That may mean, for some of us, not looking at the past as some Golden Age or believing that our contemporary world is an Age of Rust. Many such approaches to celebrating the continuity of the oral and aural traditions of poetry appear in Chapter 6.

1.   Bring and hear and maybe say

As a ten-minute component of a series of lessons, or as a special event, experiment with students bringing in a record of one song which they believe uses its words with feeling intelligence – where the words are important and where words and music collaborate to move the listener. Initially, it may be enough simply to hear and accept the music, perhaps with the briefest of comments by the introductory team. This is a preliminary to fuller discussion later, but it is worth being fairly low-profile at first. You are asking people to show their tastes in words and music, and that can make them vulnerable. It is worth waiting until a class has developed a level of trust and support before seeking an extended discussion which involves people beyond the initial group. It can be useful to commission small groups to decide what they want to introduce. Their working together should iron out a lot of potentially negative discussion within the class, reduce the amount of material to be considered and equip the students with views to share when they do present their choices.

The next stage leads to a discussion of what the students have chosen to contribute, with everyone exploring how far the words are poetry in themselves or are made effective because of their symbiotic relationship with the music. This can lead to a discussion of how far the poet and the musician have co-created the music/words. Poetry is not always or necessarily the work of a solitary mind, and this is one way of using the students' materials to see how extensively poetry is (and has been) a collaborative act as well.

2.   Bring and hear and say – taping

This approach involves pupils importing poetry into the classroom. For example, students may make a tape centred on a particular topic, for presentation to others. A small group of third formers decided to produce a tape of war poetry, using one of the group's skills as a drummer to produce appropriate sound. Interestingly, the group grew away from simple militarism as it read increasingly widely to make its five-minute tape. The readers commissioned their drummer to create moods as well as machine-guns – of sorrow and loss as much as anger and aggression. By professional standards the result was not impressive, but the tape was a genuine instance of students introducing their choice of poems to the classroom in a way that they had decided on and developed. This technique encourages groups to explore their own choices and responses, and leads naturally to an exploration, through interviews, of what others' tastes are.

3.   Interviews

Encourage groups to make tapes of poems that other people like. For instance, staff might be interviewed for their choice of poem or song. Ideally, prepare your colleagues or any other interviewees beforehand. This precaution removes any potential for shock or confusion and gives them time to think of some material. It also enables you to suggest tactfully how much time on tape they will have in which to discuss with the interviewing group why they have made their particular choice. This approach signals that poetry does not occur only in English lessons; that teachers outside 'English' like poetry; and that it is natural to chat about responses. A variation is to interview people about their favourite bad verse or about their pet hates. (One splendid 'bad' poem, for instance, is Tennyson's *Second Song to the Owl*. Any poem which begins with 'Thy tuwhits are lull'd I wot' should be worth looking at!) An extension of this scheme is for students to interview people other than teachers. School governors can make an interesting group, but, better still, there are many groups beyond school.

4.   Poems and occasions

The thematic approach is a useful one, and there are many circumstances in which you and students can produce anthologies in sound to fit a particular theme. The topical approach is less popular at secondary school level than it is at primary, but there is no reason why it should be. There are difficult and complex poems about events as well as simple ones!

The calendar is full of special occasions. Some are 'natural' such as the first day of a season. Some are culturally made, from Christmas or the Chinese New Year to the last day of the Summer Term. Pupils can be asked to form groups, each group producing a tape for a particular date assigned to it. The official first day of Winter can lead to a selection of poems and songs on The Cooling Year. November 11th can lead to a presentation on War and Peace, and so on. Students can also be asked to identify special occasions. The less facetious class will find dates, events and significances that the teacher might pass by – the start of the cricket or tennis season, the anniversary of the death of Bob Marley, the start of the United Nations 'Year of...'. Over the course of a school year, it should be possible for each small group to produce and present a selection of poems for others to listen to, as a five-minute celebration of the topicality that they have chosen. Looking at the poems and working further on them is also an option which can be pursued.

5.   Poems to relax to

Every teacher is used to the tidy start, ragged finish lesson. The pupils start in unison, but the last fifteen minutes see the inevitable hands go up as people claim to have finished. Some of them are sent back to revise their work or extend it, but others have genuinely completed their task and have some moments to spare. Often, they are told to read a book, and some do enjoy this brief encounter with a tale. An alternative is to allow some of these people to see if they find listening to poetry tapes equally rewarding and, in a serious sense, relaxing. Poetry should not always be the object of earnest concentration! There are times when, because we are half-attending, the poem can slip beneath our guard and approach us subliminally, tangentially, and in unexpected ways. You need to be well organised, and it is worth running this tactic on a small scale, at least initially. Tapes need to be clearly labelled and secure. Tape-playing gear needs to be small, robust and also secure. Personal stereo tape-playing equipment with individual headsets can be useful. The same approach may be used in a different setting, such as the Library.

6.   Library and listening

It may be more practical, in terms of cost and security, to keep most recordings in the Library's Listening Centre. Just as some people enjoy listening to a novel on tape, some enjoy listening to poetry, with or without music. It is well worth having professional recordings. Some may be to relax to. Some may have a more serious critical purpose. For instance, hearing the American poet Sylvia Plath read her poems gives them a richness of sound and an urgent intensity which a male or British voice could never hope to imitate. Any senior student considering her poetry, or that of Philip Larkin, for example, will respond the more powerfully for having heard the poem in the poet's voice. As for performance poets, who rely on sound to celebrate their poetry – from Dylan Thomas to the Afro-Caribbean rhythms and cadences of Edward Brathwaite – their voices have to be heard.

Records are expensive and vulnerable. Tapes are less likely to be damaged, but the librarian will need to devise a practical issuing system, even when tapes are made available on a reference basis. *Audiocassettes* by M. Greenhalgh, published by the School Library Association, is a brief, sensible introduction on how to extend the Library's stock of aural literature as well as literature in print (see Appendix 3).

If recordings are expensive, so, alas, are poetry books. There will be problems of expense and accessibility as you set out to match texts and tapes or records. In any case, it is a patient student who will use some system of cross-referencing to track down a poem in a book as well as a poem on a tape. An alternative is to invite skilled readers to tape poems that appear together in a particular anthology, so that a student can have access to both easily and quickly. Another, if your school obtains the appropriate copyright leave, is to copy out the poems from the tape and place tape and texts in a box together. Usually, however, it is cheaper to use your texts and have the tapes made from their choice of poems.

7. Beach head cassettes

Schools contain many readers so weak that they have difficulty in coping with 'ordinary' reading, even with the more obvious and expected structure of a story and the space it has in which to describe characters and develop relationships and events. To these students, a poem's terse presentation of a few words in an unusual layout on the page may be even more daunting, especially when the language may be playing particular, distinctive games. Brevity does not necessarily equal simplicity! This is where a good reading on tape, with an introduction and, perhaps, a running commentary, can help some students to see that a poem is not impossible, is not impenetrable and is not simply an exercise by a linguistic show-off.

Such tapes (and accompanying texts) can help students of all abilities, for being 'less able' may not necessarily be a matter of intelligence. A tape on T.S. Eliot or Ted Hughes may be as appropriate an aid for an insecure early sixth former as a tape of simpler poems for a twelve-year-old with a reading age of ten. Being 'less able' can also be a matter of cultural experience. Robert Frost's *Stopping by Woods on a Snowy Evening* may be fairly accessible to a fourth or fifth year, for example, but it will be all the more so when students hear it read in an American voice, with an exploration of the nature of winter in New England, and perhaps with a couple of personal reminiscences to help make the poem's setting and its significance accessible. Wordsworth's *Daffodils* benefits from the same approach and might avoid the problem which led Inuit (Eskimo) children to draw blue flowers. The same approach helps provide living contexts for pupils who have not encountered, for example, the culture, preoccupations and language cadences of the industrial north or of British urban West Indian culture. In such instances, a tape can help provide a context which is different from a set of pictures and may well be much richer, much more helpful. The BBC has had an honourable history of broadcasting poetry for schools. It is always worth checking its lists and making tapes of them, especially of any with a thematic approach.

Poems around the place: sights

The oral tradition of recording and celebrating poetry has been an important one and is being restored, thanks to modern technology. It is good to be able to share poetry so extensively through sound. At the same time, we can use our visual skills extensively. The invention of writing and printing has not only helped preserve much poetry. The markings made on the flat surface of the page have also become a significant part of the 'message' for many poets, some of whom deliberately play with layout as an exploratory and communicative device. Some of this playing is conventional, such as separating off the lines of a chorus in a hymn or writing a long, squiggly poem to embody a poem about a snake or a goats' mountain path, but poets have the right to play any visual game that they wish. Handling the visual approach to poetry is described in greater detail in Chapter 8. This section suggests exploiting pupils' natural sense of the visual to make poems as commonplace and open to view as other visual devices which seek their attention. This is not advocating poems as wallpaper; it is advocating poems as paper on walls to catch the eye, the head and the heart.

1.   Poster poems

Most poetry books are very conventional in their presentation of their contents. The text is usually neat and small, although it is good to see some Canadian anthologies which are prepared to give poems big titles, often in a striking type-face, and to present the poems themselves in distinctive, large print. Poster poems are a useful means of unlocking poems from books and making them attractive visually, so that people will look at the images the poem has conjured up in someone's responsive mind and will look at the text which did so. The idea, in its simplest form, is to produce a drawing, painting or collage which acts as a commentary or partner to the poem which should also appear on the same sheet of paper. The work can be as small and intense as one of William Blake's engravings, but many pupils prefer to work on a grander scale, some filling a full sheet of display card or paper. Poster poems can be created by individuals, in response to their personal choice of poems. They can also be a focus for collaborative work: a group may arrange a collage of illustrations to comment on a poem, or may choose poems to act as a collage to illuminate a particular picture. Pictures can come from any source – drawn by students or collected from magazines and newspapers. The important point is that this gives young people the chance to contribute poems and imagistic responses for others to see. They are the bringers. Poster poems are a classic example of an approach which is used in elementary education and can be used in the sixth form – a task which bridges school levels and which can challenge and involve anyone at her or his level of ability and maturity.

This approach is also a means of making sure that poems are sometimes encountered beyond the English lesson. It should involve liaison with the Art staff. It can involve collaboration with other colleagues – in Drama, History, Social Studies, the Sciences. (A class looking at poetry on seashells involved Maths staff on the mathematics of curves and spirals.) The posters can be displayed outside the English classroom. In some schools, it is possible to display poster poems in corridors, alongside other artwork; in others, a safer area, such as the Library, may be the best public place. Professionally produced poster poems are available, ranging from Rudyard Kipling's *If* to work by contemporary poets. These should be seen as a complement to those produced by students rather than a substitute for them.

2. Snippetry

Poster poems are a large-scale means of 'freeing' poetry visually from within a book. Its less grand version is 'snippetry', bringing attention to any striking use of language, no matter how small. Students may keep a private commonplace book, a little notebook in which to jot down any moments of language which particularly strike them, ranging from items they meet in poems or the press to their own inventions, arising perhaps from an exercise on kennings – one student, for instance, called a winter tree a 'sky beseecher' – or work on likenesses ('The furious kitten rose on its hydraulic legs.'). Ideally, staff and students come to share items from their collections. One teacher encourages students to identify with asterisks two or three exceptional snippets each month, to be copied out for duplication on the Star Words sheet for distribution across classes. In the case of less confident students, it may be useful to star the occasional moment in their own writing, to give them the confidence that they themselves write imaginatively and figuratively and that their profferings are worth inclusion. One or two brave teachers use a graffiti board as a means of interleaving effective expression by published poets and their students. There is the obvious danger of somebody being silly, but that can usually be sorted out. The other problem is a little more difficult – that of students coming to believe that poetry can operate only through striking verbal novelty. That can be countered by the choice of poetry that you introduce, and accepting at least a temporary enthusiasm for novelty can show pupils that poets are not afraid of using all the resources they can lay their hands on, of harnessing new ways of 'saying' to cope with their new ways of seeing, of experimenting, of bending and even breaking rules, of making up their own, and being as free as they choose. Realising that poetry is about intellectual and emotional freedom and courage, about being serious and about being playful, can arise from a judicious use of snippetry, especially when the resources include the students' own profferings.

3. Display

It is sometimes saddening to see Plato ignored in his belief that encounters with beauty can affect people positively. As encounters with excellence, some schools are architecturally catastrophic. Making them more pleasing can be hard, or almost impossible, but there is evidence to suggest that a school which perseveres with displaying works of art does promote a more humane and optimistic climate. If you are lucky, corridors, classrooms and the library can all be used for displaying poetry, regardless of who has produced it or selected and interpreted it. Poems and poster poems by pupils; poem cartoons; displays of new poetry books; class displays of poems by a particular poet or poems on a theme; displays of objects and linked poems – the room for being flexible and inventive is considerable.

The school library may have the most display space and may be the best place for presenting poems chosen or made by various years on the same topic or for the same purpose. It is possible to ensure that other students in the school look at these displays, but it is sad how often they are neglected by outsiders. Open Evening sees parents hunting down work by their own children – and then ignoring that by other students. Involving the students in setting up and advertising the display can help, as can the use of as much visual material as possible. An accompanying tape-recording of readings from the material on display can also be useful. Senior forms might generate a tape/slide sequence of people reading the poems on show, incorporating images they have chosen to accompany the poems. None of these devices ensures an attentive audience from beyond the school, but they may help.

There are also some public places which are occasionally prepared to accept such displays – the town hall, the local library, sometimes a commercial site. It is worth talking to local teachers or teacher advisers about any such places and their sympathetic contacts.

4. The classroom resource centre

Classrooms are full of resources, and there are several ways of ensuring that poems are among them. One, where copyright rules allow, is to develop collections of single copies of poems which a particular year has chosen or responded to and which it would want its successors to have the chance to meet. These can be mounted on a standard-sized card with the poem on one side, and a space on the other for pupils to write, 'I/We liked this poem because...'. Either side may be illustrated, and these poem cards can be used simply for relaxation or for further study.

Single copies of books of poems can also be useful. For less confident pupils, anthologies are probably better than *The Collected Poems of...*, for they are little resource centres in their variety of contents and are more likely to encourage 'mere' browsing. Most people who like poetry like to browse and any chance that we can provide for browsing without obligation should be exploited to the full. Anthologies should not be the only resource available, at least for senior students, since books containing poems by a single poet can be a different but even richer source for browsing. Such books may be expensive, and you may need to refer students to the school's main library or even to a sympathetic library outside.

Class libraries can also house small sets of poetry books for use by groups. This investment in four or five copies of any particular title has the advantage that you can occasionally afford to buy a sub-set which students have chosen after looking through inspection copies. Another is that sub-sets help you to break the class up into smaller groups. Each group can be set a task in which they are bringers of poems to the whole class. 'OK, I'd like each group to look for poems on happiness and sadness, one on each emotion, and which they'd like the rest of the class to listen to and look at over the next few weeks.' At other times groups may just wish to browse – poetry without obligation. Sub-sets can also be used across years. The teacher, for example, commissions pupils in one year to identify poems for another year. 'My thirteen-year-olds are into thrillers and chillers at the moment. See if you can find any poems which might appeal to them.' Any device which has students sharing in the task of choosing poems for their own further consideration or for others to experience encourages them to take some responsibility for the poetry climate in the school.

Poems around the place: workshops

Getting students to discuss and identify poems for a younger audience is only one example of a workshop in action. Most of the ideas in this chapter involve students themselves in the process of choosing, introducing, discussing and defending poems. But the idea of workshops can be extended beyond the school locality. In Geography or History, for example, the field trip is a common workshop feature which involves making as well as interpreting.

English field trips tend to take the form of an occasional visit to the theatre or the cinema, largely conducted in an interpretive mode. But there are alternatives. For example, a perennial and cross-cultural theme is that of the poet and the landscape. Ted Hughes's poetry, in his volume *Season Songs*, is one instance of the theme 'Man' and 'Nature'. Many poets draw on their native or acquired roots, or on an alienation from them. A field trip with a poet to her or his area is a particularly effective way of introducing students to the way poems grow from places. A 'good' poet, in this context, is not necessarily a great one. It is somebody you can afford and who you can rely on to stretch all the people on the field trip – maybe by visiting and introducing the contexts in which poems arose, better still by 'sketching' impressions in poetry as the visit goes on, and, best of all, by encouraging the students as well to 'sketch' verbally their responses to the place. Your regional Arts Association should be able to help you with cash and advice, but ask around as well. Not all poets belong to their area's Writers in Schools Scheme. Other schools, your English Adviser or Teacher's Centre Warden should be able to tell you of poets who are likely to enthuse you and your students – and which ones won't.

You have two main options for field trips. The first is to explore the immediate and known neighbourhood, to make it the object of vision and revision. One poet, for example, starts with an awareness exercise in which he has students blindfolded and asks them to smell their way around the school, to make them realise just how little sight contributes to their sense of place. The other option is to move to somewhere new, to explore the insights which can come from comparing the known with the unfamiliar. This can be an occasion for inter-school liaison. For example, a rural school and an urban school can play host to one another, or a multicultural school can link with one which has a more limited cultural context. The logistics of a two or three day visit can be tricky, but even a day spent in another context, if it is properly handled, can be worthwhile. At their best, such schemes encourage both home-based and incoming students to share the same experience, as they visit places and try to re-create images and moods on paper or tape, in the company of their teachers and a visiting poet.

At a senior level, students working on a particular poet or theme may well benefit from a field trip. Poets of the natural landscape such as Dylan Thomas or D.H. Lawrence or Kevin Crossley-Holland obviously provide opportunities here, but so do urban poets. And so do poets who focus on a particular point, such as those who have created the folksong of a region or the protest poetry for a particular cause. 'Dead' poets can be seen to live in what is left of the environment that affected their poetry. Living ones can be viewed in their actual context. Incidentally, 'context' should include the speech context as well as the physical environment, such as trees or canals or underground trains. The speech of an area – its idiom and cadence – may well be equally important in creating a sense of the place. As always, it is worth seeking help from organisations such as regional Arts Associations, libraries and Tourist Information Offices.

Poems around the place: the big event

The 'Big Event' can be as large or small as you want it to be. It is any occasion when poetry is seen as a chance for public celebration. One class had a sponsored Silly Verse Lunchtime Read-In for charity. One school has a poetry competition judged by a local poet, the winner being a class rather than an individual. Another has a Lazy Afternoon in late summer when each class is entitled to spend a double lesson out of doors with cokes and crisps, and with poems which have been prepared over two weeks. Senior students can enjoy creating a Words and Music evening – St. Valentine's Day is a good date. They may also enjoy co-producing a grander event with the Parent

Teachers' Association, using their own, local and imported talent. One rural school created an evening celebrating the folklore, song and poetry of the locality. Another school celebrated, in a West Indian evening, a culture with which it was not familiar – a mixture of entertainment and challenge. It was no idle entertainment but an event which gave parents, teachers and senior students much to share, and much to feel and think about. As part of a general 'Poems Around the Place' policy, linking school and home to another community, it was a one-off success. Making it less novel and creating continuity for that experience remains a challenge for that school to pursue. The notion of exploration and continuity in thought and feeling is what creating a positive climate for poetry is all about.

Finally, it is worth linking up with other schools and interested people to produce a really grand event which runs over several days. In Norfolk, for instance, teachers, advisers and lecturers from the local university's School of Education work together every two years to produce a week of activities concerned with poetry. PAN (Poetry Around Norfolk) changes according to its personnel and what they believe will appeal to people. The event involves poetry-making workshops outside school, with pupils from various schools meeting one another and working with practising poets. It is an occasion for displays of poster poems from across the county. In addition, there is a festive evening in a local theatre, with 'live' poets who are nationally known. Poets also work with senior students on how to read poetry and what the sound of a poem has to tell.

One event involved a hall floor being covered with the end of newsprint rolls, donated by a local newspaper, and a large map of Norfolk was drawn on it. Primary school pupils from across the county wrote collaborative poems about their villages and towns; these were placed on their sites on the map, which was then covered in heavy duty clear polythene sheeting (which a teacher obtained from a friendly builder). When pupils came for a half-day's workshop during PAN they could walk across the Norfolk that they had created. It was impressive to see how many people did read poems other than their own. Perhaps teachers and pupils are more generous in looking at others' poems – or perhaps we should put poems on the floor more often!

4

Reading poetry – quietly

There is an increasing awareness in education of the value of collaboration. You can see it, for example, in the notion of a pupil 'conferencing' with peers and teacher, in order to develop writing skills. It is present in the idea of groups of pupils writing class novels and in the increasing practice of collaborative writing on a word processor. There has also been considerable advocacy for the shared reading of novels, with pupils working together to pool their insights and responses. This is a theme we echo elsewhere in this book, acknowledging the public origins of much poetry and its shared exploration and celebration. But not all poetry was written to be read out loud before a large audience; not all readers of poetry would wish to be in public when they encounter a poem. There are occasions when a reader chooses to be alone. We should respect this and provide a climate in which a pupil can experiment as a private interpreter of a poem. Knowing when to offer such privacy makes demands on your skill and sympathetic awareness, but allowing pupil and poet to listen to one another is important. As Robert Bridges recognised in 'When Death to either shall come', there are times when the heart sings to the child on one's knee and times when it is better 'to read to thyself alone / the songs that I made for thee'.

Most poetry is not written for schools or for school anthologies. It is bought by readers who want to be quiet and who want to be on their own, engaging in 'productive silence'. If that is a natural way for adult readers of poetry, then we should provide for it in school as well.

Poetry as private venture

Reading poetry on one's own is a venture, with all the potential for excitement – and for worry – that the word implies. If anything, the potential for both is greater when reading poetry than when reading a prose story on one's own. For a start, a poem tends to be shorter; if it does contain a story line, it is likely to be suggested rather than stated, and so there is much more 'filling-in-the-gaps' to do.

Because most poems are relatively brief, they rely not only upon the unstated or hinted at; they also tend to use language more densely and resonantly than prose. Reading a poem can be like being a detective, tracking forwards, backwards and sideways, tracing the pattern of clues and experience. The critic, William Empson, once said that all the reasons, motives and intuitions which cause a poet to write a poem in a particular way are latent in the words – and these meet all the reasons, motives and intuitions which the reader brings along. We are never quite sure which items in the resulting richness of encounter to make the most prominent. We want them all, if we are mature and positive readers, probably enjoying the insecurity and energy which are released by what Empson calls 'the machinations of ambiguity', which he saw as being among 'the very roots of poetry'. That young man with whose words we opened this book knew what Empson was talking about, when he said that a poem is a set of words with a riddle in the middle – and it was something he seemed to relish.

But how far can being on one's own help to bring about that willing acceptance of ambiguity, resonance, call it what you will, especially when you are young and inexperienced? What approaches might help? A key point is that the teacher has to be patient and relaxed in any encouragement offered to a pupil. If being on his or her own does not prove fruitful for a particular pupil, perhaps some other approach will. Maybe she or he will grow into appreciating a little quiet later on, but not quite yet.

1. Reading frequently

Frequency and continuity are increasingly seen as key components in developing any skills and attitudes. They are certainly features of our learning to walk and talk, and the idea of a frequent, even daily focus on writing, for example, has been championed as one of the most important ways of developing competence and confidence.

The same applies to poetry. If it appears on the agenda only once a week, normally as a 'big' event, then it is given a particular status. 'It's Thursday, it's ten past two, it must be poetry' is an odd way of looking at a language activity which people of all cultures have engaged in since civilisation began! There may be times when this approach is justified, but it cannot be the only one. There should be lots of occasions when young people can just pick up a poetry book or a poetry tape and get on with it.

2. S.S.R.

As part of the school timetable 'S.S.R.' – Sustained, Silent Reading – certainly seems to create the sort of competence and confidence in reading prose that we would also like to see in reading poetry. Direct transfer of this scheme to the reading of poems may not be straightforward, but the most obvious base is to have available a stock of poetry as described in the previous chapter – poetry by individual poets, general and thematic anthologies, poetry posters and poetry tapes produced commercially and from within the school itself by other pupils and staff. Given proper display and supported by a simple borrowing system, these can be the base for the two most typical kinds of private reading, 'focused' reading and 'rummaging'.

3. Focused reading

Focused reading is based on prior knowledge. It is typical of the older student who, for example, has read some novels by D.H. Lawrence and wants to see what his poetry is like; of the twelve-year-old who is working on 'Space' and would like some poems on the topic; of the fifteen- or sixteen-year-old who is working on a theme of 'Protest' as part of her Open Study work and looking at material from the street ballad to poetry from South Africa or South America – or from the contemporary 'Babylon' of Britain itself. Your advisory role may be made harder, if you do not have many poems on the required topic. It is made easier, if you can point your client in appropriate directions – and senior pupils can be at least partly self-directing. An information network among your staff colleagues, ideally linked to a card-index system, will help the independent focused reader to find poetry much more efficiently. One school has links with its local library and encourages senior pupils to use its staff and stocks to research more widely.

4. Rummaging

Rummaging is much more general. It is the sort of independent reading which is most likely to arise from any attempt to promote frequent reading. 'OK, you have ten minutes left, so why not dip into something from the poetry area?'; or, 'We agreed last week that we would set aside twenty minutes in the next two English lessons just to browse through some poetry quietly and find what we could use for next half term, so now's the time to do just that.' For some children, this will be a chance to be quiet for a while and to browse through some poetry without being called to account.

It is useful to encourage this sort of open-ended meeting with poetry. It signals that reading quietly is natural, that it can be pleasant and need not be threatening, especially if the teacher is seen to settle down to some reading as well. Informal chat about who found what, who liked which poem, who had a thin time of it, can arise from these moments of quiet attentiveness. Such 'gossip' is an essential means for many of us of shaping an immediate response in a safe way and should be encouraged.

Some pupils will respond quickly and positively to the offer of reading space. Others may find that having to look at 'all that language written in those odd ways' is something of a switch-off. They may well find the process more amenable if they are allowed to gossip quietly at the same time – an interweaving of silence while they rummage with quiet reading and chatting to one another.

5.   Reading quietly

It is important that any occasion when pupils are genuinely reading privately should be just that – it should be their own, a time to relax into concentration without the threat of being called to account. If there is a sense of privacy and a feeling that a pupil can share what he or she has found but does not have to, a reader is more likely to settle down to experiment and explore. That means having three 'spaces' – the 'space' provided by a range of materials from which to read; the 'space' provided by time; the 'space' in which to be physically comfortable. Unfamiliarity with such an open approach will motivate some pupils; others will find the procedure discomforting and pointless. On the assumption that the pupils who enjoy the process will get on with making an extended and pleasurable encounter with poems, the rest of this chapter looks at those who will not. What to do with those who see privacy as isolation? How do we encourage them to 'grow' towards seeing it as an opportunity instead?

Training for independence

The most natural approach is to move away from absolute privacy. Where appropriate, set up paired rummaging or focused browsing. Harness the natural inclination to chat to tasks where quietness and occasional silence are also seen as components. Build in yourself as someone who wants to read poems and who, sometimes, wants to read them out, wants to hear them read, wants to talk about them and to listen to what others have to say. This sort of quiet, informal but reflective sharing can be for some the slope into private reading as a pleasurable activity. Its main virtue is its flexibility: the sharers, including you, can feel when it's right to be silent and private. As the 'wise adult', your role in such sharing may be different from that of a peer, involving you more as a consultant. Less secure and motivated pupils may call upon your greater knowledge of poetry and of the resources available in your room and elsewhere. You may also have some knowledge of a pupil's particular interests, enthusiasms and worries. Suggesting possible poems to pupils is not, to use the horrid phrase, some form of 'bibliotherapy', but it may be the means of getting them to introduce themselves to one another. So, some chatting and sharing with you as well as with peers may be a way in for some. There are other approaches which can supplement it.

1.   Providing entry – tapes

There are some readers who do not hear a poem when they read it. Others hear it without realising the contribution that a poem's sound makes to its potential richness. This is where a tape recorder can be valuable, since it brings the poem to the ear, even when the reading is accompanied by the printed text. There are some excellent readings of poetry. It is certainly worth buying some tapes as a school resource, perhaps basing some of them in the Library Listening Centre. At senior level, for instance, anyone studying

Sylvia Plath's poetry needs to hear the urgency which her voice, with its particular pronunciation and cadence, gives to such poems as *Daddy*. The strong discipline in Eliot's reading of his *Four Quartets* or the complex sad–happy quality of John Betjeman reading his own poetry signals to the reader how the poet saw and heard the poems. Similar readings can establish beach heads of understanding for young readers as well.

Tapes can take other forms (readings by actors, for example), but consider school-produced tapes as well, especially where a particular poet is not available on tape. Recruit the best staff voices in the school; use senior pupils; occasionally there is a fine, sympathetic reader to be recruited from among parents; you might find a local actor ready to read Henry Treece's *Conquerors* and other poems for your own tape on, for instance *War and Peace*. Produce readings which are fairly brief – three or four key poems by one poet or four or five poems on a theme. Cross-reference the tape and the original texts, so that a pupil can hear the one and see the other and think about how the two have been linked.

2. Providing entry – illustration

One other gateway to independence is through the visual. For a start, it is worth investing in anthologies which successfully and evocatively juxtapose picture and poem, so that pupils can explore the links and tensions created. They can respond in various private ways, perhaps by keeping comments in their reading logs, by identifying their own choice of illustration, or by discussing their response with a friend. It is also worth looking out for poetry posters. These have become less popular, but some are still available. Certainly, old stalwarts such as Kipling's *If* and the *Desiderata* can be bought, often as examples of calligraphy. Ideally, you are seeking large-scale illustrations in which the poem is echoed and enriched.

3. Signposting

Poetry books can be off-putting. For example, a book filled with poems by one writer involves the problem of where to start; a general anthology can look like a confusion; a thematic anthology has some sort of structure, but it may not chime with a reader's perceptions of themes. Signposting possible routes through such selections can help less secure readers. It is probably best done through informal consultancy, through talking. Other approaches might be considered:

1. You can set up systems by which pupils can track down poems which others of their age have liked. For instance, you can have a card-index system or a wall-chart series which identifies poems which have appealed to previous twelve-year-olds; or which appealed to thirteen-year-olds looking at the topic of Heroes and Heroines; or which acted as back-up to a senior class exploring a particular time, such as poets of the Second World War, as an examination coursework option.

2. You can set up systems by which pupils recommend poems they have enjoyed. If you are having a Poetry Rummage over half a term, pupils can jot down on a list poems they have liked. Others can then initial any entries they also like, so creating a popularity chart.

3. The brave can follow the American idea of something approaching a graffiti board on which pupils can scribble comments about poems. 'Want to read a poem about the older generation being unfair to young people? Look in *Rattlebag* page 233!' 'If you're looking for a spooky poem, see Walter De La Mare's *John Mouldy*.' You will need to supervise such a board and may need to prime it with a few suggestions at the start, so that pupils get the idea of the 'come on' style that you are after. In fact, starting up your 'Recommended' board in the first place can be the occasion for requiring everyone to find a poem.

    Items 2 and 3 can form the basis for rummaging with the following year's classes of the same age and can be used to discuss how tastes have altered or stayed the same.

4. If you do not mind the slight mutilation involved, pupils can put a small peel-off sticker against a poem in an anthology they have liked (one per reader and no more than five in all) so that insecure rummagers can see that certain poems have appealed to previous pupils of their age and therefore might appeal to them as well. The aim is to find ways of reducing the confrontation which a mass of unfamiliar poems can set up in the mind of the uncertain reader.

4. Staying with the poem

Be careful about this. Quite often, your aim is simply to get pupils to relax among poems. Achieving that can sometimes be quite a triumph. Do not rush matters by insisting on deeper, extended reading too soon, especially when you receive pupils from your intake schools. There will be some pupils who will want to stay with a poem and it can be worth providing opportunities for them to do so. Again, these will grow best out of the pupil's own ideas or from discussing them with someone else – a peer or teacher.

There are other approaches which can supplement such informally negotiated activity. One is to produce a *POSSIBILITIES* card with a set of possible activities arising from poems. For example, one class included the following piece from the Bible's Ecclesiastes in its selection for fourteen-year-olds, since several pupils were moved by its balanced rhythms and images.

> To every thing there is a season, and a time to every purpose under the heaven;
> A time to be born, and a time to die; a time to plant, and a time to pluck up that which is planted;
> A time to kill, and a time to heal; a time to break down, and a time to build up;

A time to weep, and a time to laugh; a time to mourn, and a time
to dance;
A time to cast away stones, and a time to gather stones together;
a time to embrace, and a time to refrain from embracing;
A time to get, and a time to lose; a time to keep, and a time to cast
away;
A time to rend, and a time to sew; a time to keep silence, and a
time to speak;
A time to love, and a time to hate; a time of war, and a time of
peace.

Now that makes a splendid passage for a class to work on, to produce a
reading, maybe with sound effects and appropriate music. It is also an
example of something which an individual can read and return to. Here are
some options that can be presented on a *POSSIBILITIES* card:

1. *That writing comes from the 'Authorised Version' of the Bible and is
    written in the English of over 350 years ago. Borrow a tape recorder
    and read it fairly slowly on to the tape. Then read it much faster, as if it
    were a piece of modern English. Which do you prefer? You could try
    to sort out your reasons and note them in your personal reading log.*

2. *That was a translation of the original Jewish text. See if a Jewish friend
    will read it to you in her or his language. Listen to its 'music'. You
    could discuss how far the sounds of the reading told you what it was
    about.*

3. *Compare the 1611 'Authorised Version' translation that you first read
    with a modern one. (Your teacher will help you to find a modern
    version.) You could compare what the differences are on the page –
    changes of words, for instance. Then you could read the modern
    translation on the tape and listen to your two readings. You could
    compare the two and comment on which version you like better in
    your reading log – or maybe even produce your own version.*

4. *The 1611 version doesn't have rhyme or rhythm like an ordinary
    poem, but it doesn't feel like 'ordinary' prose either. What makes it
    different for you? You could try writing three or four 'verses' like it on
    a topic of your own choosing. If you can't think of one, have a chat
    with a partner. Maybe you could compose some on school life, or the
    life of an animal, or a job that someone close to you does, or the
    seasons of the year. Produce your own version, trying to remain
    faithful to the style and seriousness of Ecclesiastes. Jot it in your
    personal writing collection – or produce it as an illustrated text – or
    put it on tape.*

5. *Produce the script for a class reading of the 1611 version, using
    musical notation – f for loud, pp for very quiet, cresc. for getting
    louder, and so on. (This is a chance to look up music notation in an*

encyclopaedia or to have a brief consultation with a music teacher.)
Then write a few lines about why you want it read in that way. If it's
possible, get together with a few friends and try it out.

6. *Produce a poster, maybe a collage, to catch the mood of all or part of*
    the 1611 version.

So far, each item has been designed for the reader to stay within the text as
well as move, sympathetically, outside it. Each item has tried to have the
reader focus and rummage at the same time. Not all private readers want to
work this way. Some will want to respond by 'springboarding' – using the
poem as a means of jumping off into a responsive narrative. That is often
typical of younger and less secure readers. You can cater for these quite
simply:

7. *Take one of the pairs of 'times' that the passage tells you about, such*
    as: 'A time to keep silence, and a time to speak'. Tell a story based
    upon it. It might be about something which actually happened. It
    might be a story you invent.

Finally, a few may want to read more in the same genre or style, or more by
the same poet. In this instance, references to the Authorised Version of the
Bible's account of Earth's creation (*Genesis 1*) or Christ's Sermon on the
Mount (*Matthew 5*) or, for senior pupils, the love poetry of *The Song of
Solomon, Chapter 4* could encourage some to enjoy more of the rhetoric and
sonorousness of this particular literary resource.

The above is an example of a *POSSIBILITIES* card provided by a teacher
for a pupil to select items from. Groups of pupils can become quite interested
in producing such cards for poems which they have 'adopted', designing the
cards for other groups in the class or for younger pupils in the school.

5. Guidelines

You may feel insecure about such an open agenda – or believe that some of
your pupils will. In that case, you might wish to provide a slightly more
explicit structure, to promote attention. The guidelines suggested here could
be the basis for a set which you adapt and produce to suit your particular
pupils. In this instance, assume that Henry Treece's poem *Conquerors* is
being explored. (You will find the complete text in Appendix 1a.)

1. *If you can, use a copy of the poem which you can place in the middle*
    of a large-ish sheet of paper. If you can't, then place a sheet of paper
    alongside the poem.
2. *The important thing about a poem is not to make your mind up*
    about it too early. So take your time. Relax and explore.
3. *Read the whole poem, just to get the general idea of it. Don't worry if*
    it is not making much sense at this stage.
4. *Now see if it has a title. If it does, draw a spidergram from it and jot*
    down anything that it brings to mind. For example, the title
    Conquerors *might have you thinking like this:*

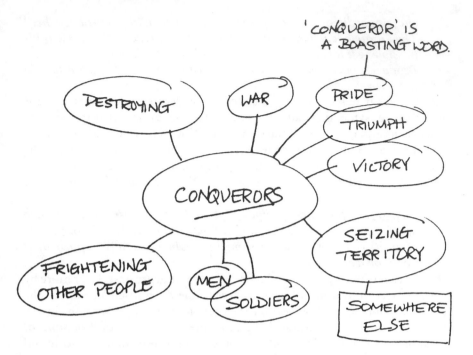

5. Read the poem again and see if any of the things you wrote in your spidergram start to help you understand the poem. If it's possible, draw link-lines between your spidergram and anything which seems related in the poem.

6. It can be worth reading the poem more than once – that includes a reading which you can hear inside your head or one recorded on a tape for you to listen to. Seeing the poem and hearing the poem could both be telling you things about it.

7. Even if the whole poem is not having much impact, there are likely to be bits that you notice. Jot down around the outside of the poem comments about anything which strikes you:
    *   the vocabulary
    *   the way things are said
    *   noticeable rhymes and rhythms
    *   any odd features, such as absence of punctuation
    *   the layout of the poem.

8. Now do the same for comments on anything which strikes you about these:
    *   any way in which the poem appeals to each of your senses – sight, sound, taste, touch, smell
    *   any way in which it signals emotions and moods to you.

9. *Now try to link the comments together. You can do this with coloured felt-tips, for instance. You might find that there is a lot in your poem about sound. Link the bits which are about that. There might be a lot about being happy or sad. There might be a strong use of rhyme. You could find yourself underlining or circling a part of the poem for more than one cluster of ideas. That's fine. You are seeing how a poem can carry a lot of messages at one time.*

10. *It's time to relax a moment. Go back and read the poem on its own. Now go back to all your notes and see if some of the things you have been noting are more important to you than others. Those could be the ones to follow up by writing about them in your reading log or discussing them with someone else.*

11. *It's time to bring your reading of the poem and your notes together. Ask yourself:*
    - *What sort of mood is this poem creating?*
    - *How far is that mood the result of the subject of the poem?*
    - *If there is someone speaking in the poem, is it the poet or someone she or he has invented to speak in that poem?*
    - *How far are the mood created in the poem and the mood created in me the result of how the poet wrote about the subject? What did she or he do to make me respond in that way?*
    - *What do I think the poem is telling me, making me feel and think about?*

    These five items could be used for further jottings in your reading log, or for discussion with someone else; or they could help you to work out how to read the poem aloud, or to tackle a poetry poster for it, or to write a brief essay.

12. *Always put a poem together again: read it once more and let it be. It may escape you, or it may well find its freedom by staying with you.*

6. It sounds to me ...

One school encourages pupils to work with a tape recorder and a poetry book. This is implicit, for example, in item 5 of the *POSSIBILITIES* sheet outlined earlier in this chapter. A pupil can go to a study carrel in the corner of the room, or be sent to the Library or some other fairly secluded place. As with the *POSSIBILITIES* sheet, the pupil is first asked to concentrate on how the poem might be read and to pencil down some notes on such topics as volume and pace; on using soft or thin or full or harsh voice, and so on. The next stage is for the pupil to tape the poem according to his or her own directions, to listen to the tape and to read it until the sound 'inside the head' is reproduced on the tape. The idea is that the pupil is already thinking about the poem as an experience, making that experience into sound and having a record of it to think about. The pupil is listening to his or her self interacting with the poem and has a chance to think about it, without the threat of having to write and be called to account.

The next stage is for the pupil to comment, on tape, on the printed poem and the sounded one. If possible, the pupil is encouraged to produce the commentary in the form of questions as well as statements. 'What does that bit mean where the poet talks about "night covering the pole"?' 'Why couldn't I say that line as easily as the others?' 'Why isn't there any punctuation to help me?' 'Why did I find this poem boring?' This may sound artificial, but it signals that being puzzled is good, natural and potentially positive; that asking questions is a fine starting place for a conversation; that you can harness questions to help you move on. Listening to their own questions, many pupils will start to tackle them. Ideally, they should have time to try to answer them, and to read the poem again in order to re-assemble it and see how far their thinking has reinforced or altered their original interpretation. This technique of inquiring into literature by asking questions will be developed in the final chapter 'Towards Artifact'.

You can leave matters at that. Or, you can invite pupils, occasionally, to let you listen to their tapes. (You may have to listen to the occasional tape, if you suspect unoriginal sloth, although we have not encountered much of it in response to this approach.) If several pupils have tackled the same poem on their own, you have an unusually rich basis for small-group discussion among pupils who have been prepared to share ideas. The results of working in this way are promising and provide a range of further opportunities.

7.   Presenting a challenge

If you have some pupils who like being challenged and stretched, there is no reason why you should not produce a challenging agenda of items for them to explore. The questions will depend on the pupil's competence and confidence; upon the poem; upon the aspects of response about which the pupil would like to be challenged. There is no set pattern for this. Sometimes, you might be able to provide a task sheet; quite often, the challenge will be an oral one as you discuss a poem with a pupil. 'O.K., You say you like sad poems. Here's one called *Strange Meeting* by Wilfred Owen. Now the topic's sad – being killed in a war – but some people say that the rhyme scheme makes it sound sad as well. Explore what you think they mean by that and come back to me with your views on it.'

8.   It occurs to me ...

Many of the ideas suggested elsewhere in this book can be adapted for personal reflection and response. The most obvious remains the personal log, whether it is kept as a tape or in written form. Encourage its use as a means of keeping a running commentary on what has been read, on the process of reading and on the nature of response. With younger pupils, it should be as informal a document as the pupil needs, with comments on how their reading has prospered, snatches of poems, experiments in appropriate lettering, doodles and sketches as means of visualising poems and whatever else helps the pupil to interact with a poem. There is no reason why the same catch-as-catch-can approach should be excluded from senior pupils' journals, which can include experiments in pastiche and paraphrase as means of concentrating on the poem's language.

9. Holding on to poetry

Perhaps the most important way of making poetry come alive for an individual is to encourage her or him to hold on to any poems which have been particularly valued. One way is to encourage the keeping of a 'commonplace' book or folder in which a pupil can write or place such poems. These grow into a collection   poems valued for the thought and feeling invested in them, alongside poems valued because the pupil has written them. Poems can also be made personal and permanent through taping or through artwork. Perhaps best of all is the poem inside the mind. The days of compulsorily learning poetry chosen by others have gone for most pupils. That is not the same, however, as inviting them to hold on to poems they themselves find valuable. Encouraging the learning of the occasional poem or snatch of a poem is not being destructive. It can help some pupils to own some poems for life.

None of these approaches sets out to offer an exercise in formal literary criticism. The main aim is to enable young people to learn that the private response to poetry is one which they can find comfortable and enabling – and if you are seen to enjoy poetry quietly yourself, that could be one of the most powerful motivators of all.

5

Talk

Talk as exploration

1. Classroom context

People who design the interiors of restaurants, pubs or large businesses know the importance of atmosphere in encouraging relaxed conversation. They pay close attention to colour schemes, decor, lighting, furnishings and not least to seating arrangements. It is very rare, however, that such considerations are taken into account in designing classrooms. Placing desks clearly in rows, isolating one child from another, is not an arrangement which favours relaxed conversation. Neither is having more than two children sitting side by side, nor is having the seating randomly determined by the children, so that there is perhaps one child sitting alone in a corner, one turning around to talk to the two behind, three sitting side by side, a gang of five at the back of the room. If constructive talk is to be a valued part of the curriculum, the context needs to be planned.

The overall plan for talk should allow for a balance of informal and formal structures. At the informal end of the scale, a relaxed atmosphere which encourages pupils to chat about their experiences of poetry might best be developed in the early stages through allowing pupils free choice of seating arrangements to build up their confidence. For the teacher to have an encouraging, welcoming manner will be one of the most significant factors in making the informal approach a success. Carpets, easy chairs, soft lighting may be outside your control, although some schools have found it possible to fit out part of the Library or a classroom with such things as bean-bag loungers, a length of carpet and display shelving for interesting books. Attractive wall displays of children's writing or of published pictures must be possible in most schools, and will help build a conducive context in which to chat about poetry.

Out of such informal settings will come occasions for more focused work. Where seating arrangements in a classroom are flexible, chairs should be rearranged to suit the kind of talk which you want to encourage. At times it will be most effective if children do not talk but work quietly on their own. In that case, separate individual desks would be the best arrangement. At times you may want pairs of children simply to exchange views, or perhaps to go on to work out a co-operative response; in this case pairs of seats or desks side by side will be the best solution. At times you might want groups of children to discuss a poem or prepare a reading; then, small circles of chairs or desks will allow the participants to face each other.

In addition to these possibilities you may want individuals to report back to the whole class. In that case it is worth considering how important that stage is to be and how much time it requires. That will determine whether or not the seating arrangement should be changed, since people do not like to be moved around more than once. Ask the class to revert to a previous arrangement only if it is to be for an important or lengthy phase of the lesson.

In setting the context for oral work the best results will be gained if the aims are positively and consistently affirmed. Self-determination by pupils may signal a democratic climate, but if moving into groups is accompanied by noise and disorder, it is more likely to signal that talk is not really important, and is only a period of 'socialising' before more structured activity. So, before giving the order to move, explain clearly who is to go where, for how long and for what purpose. The first time any new arrangement is tried out it may not be very smooth, but classroom procedures need to be repeated and practised to make them effective.

2. Pair work

Response to poetry is most likely to be deepened when individuals have time for thought and reflection before sharing their response through talk. Any sequence which involves talk should allow for, and even encourage, individuals to withdraw at any stage to work out their own response – although individual differences stand in the way of a hard and fast rule here. Some people, the less secure, respond positively only when they have heard the views of others first; confessing their own deeply held beliefs straight out is too close to 'the dangerous edge of things', in Robert Browning's phrase.

Pair work allows for the highest proportion of talk – fifty per cent of the class may be talking at any one time. This can make for a noisy activity, and so ground-rules need to be spelt out beforehand and reinforced during the activity when necessary. The basic ground-rule is for talk to be polite, the speaker taking a positive attitude towards the subject and the listener. The cause of excess noise can sometimes be poor listening, with supposed listeners interrupting a speaker, perhaps showing a lack of sympathy for an opposing view, with the result being a shouting match. Instead of just asserting the need for quiet by use of *force majeure*, it is worth asking a class to analyse and comment on their own performance in discussion. In spite of the risk of excess noise, pair work is valuable. It can be supportive without causing the tension which 'having to perform' before a larger number can induce in some people.

Careful pairing can allow pupils with special educational needs to be drawn into the discussion, if their partner is someone who is both sensitive and encouraging, without actually doing all the work for them. An informal note-making phase, involving only a limited amount of writing, is important for low-ability pupils, who can play a full part at this level. Some may prefer to make notes in the form of sketches or diagrams, and it is important to recognise that pupils with low ability in writing may have other better developed abilities which will serve this purpose.

For all pupils, making notes is an important skill which needs supervision and guidance. There can be a continuum of detail from single-word jottings on what has caught the attention of the pupil at the time, through a more orderly sequencing of the main points of the discussion, to a complete though abbreviated set of 'minutes'. The short term value of notes is that they commit the writer to articulating a view which can later be extended in written or oral work. The long term value of note-making is that from a basis of personal commitment individuals become accustomed to ordering and shaping their own ideas, and so develop confidence in their personal critical judgment.

3. Group work

Research by Barnes and Todd (1977) Benton (1986) and Dias (1987) has shown that teacherless groups can achieve a high level of critical analysis through free discussion of a poem and what seems important to them in it. Group structures are almost infinitely variable but there are basically four considerations which can produce a range of alternative structures:

free peer group	open agenda
role-specific group	pre-specified agenda

In the free peer group there is no demarcation of roles or responsibilities. Any person may speak at will, though of course the usual ground-rules for talk behaviour apply. Providing a tape-recorder to record the group's deliberations is a powerful stimulus, and the group can get a lot out of hearing back part of their discussion later. In the role-specific group several of the group will have specific tasks to perform, particularly the chair, scribe, and spokesperson. These roles will have a direct effect upon their speech behaviour and indirectly on the behaviour of the others in the group. Older pupils in particular might like this simulation of committee structure.

The open agenda clearly calls for a high degree of commitment and responsibility if it is to work effectively and efficiently, but because it is an activity which allows pupils to make their own meanings from the poetry, they tend to recognise it as a useful approach and co-operate accordingly. A pre-specified agenda might ask them to decipher the literal meaning of a poem, or look for patterns of metaphor, or answer specific questions.

No matter which approach is chosen, setting up groups raises the following issues:

- Who is to be in the group?
- Is there to be a chair, spokesperson and scribe?
- How long is to be allowed for each phase of the discussion?
- What are the topics for discussion?
- What has to be achieved by the end of which stage?
- What is to happen as a result of the discussion?

Even where there is an open agenda in unstructured peer groups these issues are of concern. There seems to be little advantage in keeping pupils in the dark over them and everything to be gained from a positive, problem-solving approach.

About four people is right for a group to work most efficiently. With more than that there are likely to be passengers; people can take fewer turns in talking and participants may have to shout to be heard. If the group has a chairperson, her or his role may include ensuring that there is proper 'turn-taking'. While the group may have a scribe, note-taking effectively precludes that person from taking an active part in the discussion. It is probably more genuinely useful to have everyone taking part in the discussion and in the final summarising. If the group has a spokesperson, he or she will take the lead in reporting back to the whole class what the group decided, and so needs to be able to understand the main points made by the group. When only five minutes remain of their discussion time groups should be advised to make a summary and brief their spokesperson. If a group has adopted roles, they should rotate session by session so that all the class has a chance to learn and apply the skills each role involves.

Self-selected groups are not a bad thing, but they may sometimes contain an unhelpful mixture of individuals. This relates not only to the disruptive ones. It is quite possible for pupils to be with the same comrades throughout the whole of their schooling, primary and secondary. More important, then, for the best pupils as well as the worst to encounter new ideas, new values. Some of the best pupils as well as some of the worst will be most resistant to changes in grouping, but they need to see that change can be in their own interests. Moving someone from a particular place or group is usually used as a form of punishment, which is unfortunate; so, when you intend to interrupt the usual pattern of seating or grouping it is best to do this early on in the lesson, giving notice of what the change is to be and, most importantly, explaining why. 'On this occasion I'd like you all to form different groups, so that you can all hear different points of view from usual.'

Clear instructions on what a pair or a group is to discuss can sometimes be helpful if children think that talk is not real work. If they see talk as time-wasting, not a real activity, and getting them nowhere, you might wish to provide instructions on the board or an assignment sheet for each group. Groups might need to be weaned from dependence on a teacher-led agenda to taking responsibility for exploring a poem in their own terms.

Talk tends to fill the space available, and it is probably advisable to set time limits. Absolute guidelines are impossible, given that what is to be discussed is just one of the determining factors as to how long is needed. Ten minutes may well be considered a substantial unit of time. Within any lesson though it is likely that there will be phases, within which different kinds of talk are the focus: pair work, group work and whole-class discussion. Any phase of group work may be sub-divided into shorter stretches, framed by progress reports back to the whole class. It is advisable to have the first report-back after only a short stretch of group discussion, to check that the groups are on target with the task and in their own management.

4. Whole class

The level of formality increases as the numbers involved in talk increase. It is much less demanding and threatening to talk intimately with a close friend than to hold your own in a group discussion and more demanding again to explain your views to the whole class. A gradual build-up, within one lesson, of the numbers involved in a discussion builds confidence. After the initial introductory phase of the lesson, pupils may find the following outline helpful as a standard pattern for discussion:
1. Silence in which individuals can think, reflect and jot down notes of their own ideas.
2. Sharing those ideas with a friend and developing a collaborative view.
3. Explaining the collaborative view to another pair – hence making a group of four – and forming a new collaborative view.
4. Reporting back to the whole class and engaging in open discussion of the issues raised.

5. Did you like that poem?

In any teaching, the commitment and overt enthusiasm of the teacher is considered to be one of the key factors determining success. Class management based on principles clearly understood by the pupils can reduce pressure on the teacher who should be then more free to show genuine enthusiasm for the poetry chosen. Strong commitment to the subject by the teacher can however appear restrictive, not allowing pupils the chance to make the material their own. It is important that the management of the talk encourages individual response. Beware the trap of reading a poem and then asking immediately afterwards the question, 'Did you like that?' This invites the answer, 'No!'; and the obvious follow-up of 'Why not?' invites the answer, 'It's boring'. In terms of classroom psychology, the 'Did you like it?' question is too deep and too sudden. Bloom's taxonomy of educational objectives suggests that being asked to make a value judgment is the highest level of question, and hence requires preparatory steps for an adequate response. Much better to reserve that question until the last, and spend the lesson guiding pupils towards a deeper enjoyment, beyond their initial gut-reaction. 'How does that compare with your own experience?' is perhaps a more approachable first-stage question. Thereafter use the sequence suggested above as a general guideline for proceeding towards an evaluation of the poem.

6.   Teacher questions

Questioning always plays a major part in the way teachers handle poetry, in interacting with the whole class or in setting assignments for individuals, pairs or groups. It may be helpful to see questions as belonging to three types:

1.   **Closed:** where there is a definite answer of a factual kind. Example: 'What kind of wood did Robert Frost describe in *The road not taken*? Answers will be convergent.
2.   **Open:** where there is room in the answer for individual opinion and belief. Example: 'What do you think happened next in *The Flight of the Roller Coaster*? (See Appendix 1a for this poem.) Answers will be divergent.
3.   **Enabling:** where there is an invitation to the speaker to extend an answer. Example: 'When that happened to you, did you feel the same way as the poet describes?'

There is a tendency for closed questions to be seen as of limited value — limited to the facts of who, what, when, where, why; but each of these questions has a place and a use. A poem does contain factual information, and it is as misleading to suggest to pupils that a response to literature is just a matter of opinion, as it is sterile to teach only a Gradgrind diet of facts about poetic form. It is interesting to note though that two of the three question types above allow pupils to formulate their own views. That two to one ratio of 'opinion' to 'fact' would seem to be about right and to suggest the kind of balance that a teacher leading a discussion ought to strive for.

7.   Talk to explore experience

Only a few of the pupils in any school will go on to advanced literary studies. For almost all pupils the significance of poetry lies in its relationship to life, their own and that of others. The detail of what is discussed in poetry lessons will depend in large degree on the poem itself, but there is one underlying principle: pupils will be most interested and find the material most relevant when they can relate it to life, particularly life as they see it. That is not to encourage a narrow parochialism; the best poetry has a universal significance, no matter what culture or time it comes from.

If an exploration of pupils' own experience is to be paramount, it raises the question of when in the lesson a poem should be presented to the class. The usual pattern is probably for the class to walk into the lesson and to encounter the poem as the first stage, perhaps after a brief introduction by the teacher. If our main aim is to celebrate the common experience underlying the poem rather than the poem itself, then this suggests that the first stage of the lesson should be concerned with an exploration of that experience as the pupils see it, delaying the poet's version until they have made up their own minds on where they stand. It is worth remembering that the teacher has probably had a great deal of time to think about the poem and what it means to him or her personally. Pupils within one lesson cannot come close to that kind of intimate knowledge. If presented with a poem at an early stage they will know intuitively that they are supposed to like it – why else did the teacher select it? It is a published art form, so how can they genuinely criticise it? If it is put to them before they have grappled with the experience it describes, then they have the doubly difficult task of coming to terms with the art form and what it represents, simultaneously.

The solution is to use talk to explore the experience first. Ask the class what they know and feel about it. Encourage each person to jot down notes – to create a provisional viewpoint. Let them share ideas, tell anecdotes, re-align their opinions, recreate the sensations of an experience in words. Show them pictures, use improvised drama, read related prose, have them write poetry – whatever it takes to get inside the experience. Then present the poem as one person's version of that reality. They have already formulated their own ideas about the experience so they should be able to see the poem more clearly. That is extremely important in giving them confidence in their critical judgment – especially for the pupils who will go on to advanced and even university literary studies. The discussion which follows will be more concerned to contrast the poet's vision – or more likely specific aspects of it – with their own.

This approach works particularly well with poem clusters. A cluster of poems on the same subject will offer contrasting viewpoints, and everyone should be able to find something that they can identify with. The debate which will follow, over who prefers which poem and why, will draw pupils into a more active commitment to poetry. As this approach is used over a period of time, pupils will be able to build up a personal anthology of poems with which they can identify.

8.   Assignment questions

It has been suggested so far that groups will be able to talk about a poem on their own without their attention being focused on specific 'comprehension' questions. All pupils, under certain circumstances, are capable of such open discussion – where they set the agenda of issues, with just an invitation to talk about the poem and the topics in it which they feel are important. This approach is put forward first to show its importance.

However, some groups, particularly if they are used to more teacher-directed tasks, may feel comfortable only with more specific instructions. Such questions as, 'What season of the year is the poem describing? How do you know that?' will give them a certain sense of achievement since the answers are specific and factual, even though limited. The argument against setting a series of such questions is that what the adult setting the question sees as significant may not be what pupils see as a priority, and so they are obliged to focus on aspects of the poem which may not be the most significant to them. It reinforces the perception of learning as just an academic exercise. An international research project led by Patrick Dias into teacherless groups (see Appendix 3) clearly showed that, across a whole class, groups will in any case make reference to most of the points teachers see as significant but in a framework of their own choosing. That framework will include the timing and the order of priority of any given concern. What a teacher foresees as a first order question may in fact be too difficult for some groups to take on board until late in the discussion, or of less significance than other points and so on. The psychological impact of the open agenda is very important. Such an agenda belongs to the pupils, allowing them to become committed to it and through it to the poetry. The subsequent whole-class discussion is the time to adjust their perception if necessary, but with sensitivity to their commitment.

If it is necessary to give more specific directions, it is worth considering the more open and more generally applicable kinds of question:

- What is the poet trying to describe? What can you see most clearly?
- What does the poet want you to feel?
- What seems most important to you about the poem?
- Is this like your experience in any way?
- What words or phrases catch your attention?

If you stress that these questions are only a guideline, to be taken in any order, they become a technique, a way of approaching any poem, rather than a test of pupils' success in decoding one particular poem.

Talk as performance

Reading poetry aloud to a class is an important teaching technique; it can bring a poem's meaning to life with more immediacy than any other approach and a committed performance can do a great deal to promote interest. A live reading, where the voice, face and gestures of a reader are there for the listener to focus on is a powerful form of presentation for teacher and pupils to work towards. But poetry is always in some way or other a challenge to read. Poets use techniques which are in tension one with another to heighten meaning: for instance the end of the line is often not the end of the meaning – the reader may have to take such features as *enjambement* (see Appendix 2) into account. The natural rhythm of speech and metric rhythm do not always match. Alliteration and assonance may sound ridiculous if over-stressed ... and so on.

The central question is not whether there should be frequent performance reading of poetry, but who should do it and when.

1.   Pupils reading

Pupils, too, will certainly want to read aloud and will learn a great deal about the poem and themselves if they have the opportunity to do so – but only when they have had adequate time to prepare, have had guidance in what to watch out for and perhaps the chance to practise at home or somewhere quiet, with a friend or sympathetic group to give advice. To ask pupils to read poetry to the rest of the class is to ask them to walk across a minefield. One of the most supportive approaches is for pupils to work in pairs, trying out ideas or training each other to give a particular interpretation in performance.

Meaning and form are usually bound in a complex relationship in poetry, and first acquaintance is too soon to call for pupils, no matter how keen or talented, to give a performance reading to the whole class. A good performance is always built up through rehearsals, and here the two aspects of talk in this chapter come together – because the activity of preparing a poem for performance will generate a great deal of exploratory talk in which the poem will be analysed and interpreted.

You will not want always to give a 'model' reading beforehand; that might limit their own response to a particular kind of interpretation. In the long term they will develop into confident readers if they are given general guidance on possible techniques first, then support and advice whilst rehearsing. Any commentary afterwards on what they did well and not so well should always be sympathetic. Preliminary guidelines might include the following points on preparing a reading:

1.   Work out the phrasing of the poem – for meaning and for dramatic effect.
2.   Work out the stress pattern. Which are the important words?
3.   Intonation – Does the poem have a music or a meaning which needs your voice to rise or fall, and where?
4.   What is the mood of the poem and how does this affect the way you read it?

Indirectly such preparatory work will involve close analysis of the text, covering the same ground as a traditional comprehension exercise. Preparing a poem for reading is easier if pupils can write on the text – putting bar lines for phrasing, oblique lines to show rising intonation, underlining for strong stress and so on. Different coloured marker pens can also help codify the reading. Marking the text with some code to show who reads what and how is essential, although if they are working from a school text to be used with following year-groups that might be difficult.

2. Teacher reading

Clearly the best situation is when the class teacher is unselfconscious about giving intelligently responsive readings, as often as possible, using strong intonation and stress patterns to bring out the meaning. Many teachers are unsure about their ability but, as with so many other performance skills, confidence comes with practice and self-belief. The teacher will be technically the best reader in almost any class, with rare exceptions. At the other end of the scale teachers committed to reading poetry as a performance need to allow pupils space to grow. Pupils learn to read well only by reading badly at first in a supportive climate.

3. The visiting reader

No matter how skilled the class's usual teacher, a visiting reader will have a strong appeal as a fresh stimulus. The regional Arts Associations (see Appendix 4) have an invaluable scheme for sponsoring published writers' visits to schools to give readings, to talk about their work and to run creative workshops. The visit can turn into a mini-Eisteddfod, the mere novelty of the occasion being sufficient to give poetry teaching a lift. Beyond that, the insight into the writing process which published writers give is fascinating, and helps pupils to see that they themselves are potential writers and shapers of their own experiences, not just in response to the demands of schooling. Any visit should allow time for pupils to interact with the visitor, asking questions and making comments. This will be more successful if the class discusses possible questions beforehand, and if the interaction takes place in an informal and encouraging atmosphere. For instance, to place a visitor before several classes formally seated in the school hall is probably cost-effective but puts severe constraints upon the kind of interaction possible.

Parents and people from the local community may also have a valuable contribution to make. Poetry from other cultures can be powerfully enhanced by being read in an authentic voice; Caribbean poetry, for instance, has strong rhythms and intonation patterns which are different from British English. Asian poetry comes from a centuries-old cultural background which is best explained by someone brought up in that tradition rather than by reference to a book.

4. Other performances

Regional theatres on occasion mount performances by poets, perhaps as part of an arts festival or local carnival. Actors reading an anthology can be a compelling experience, when the magic of footlights is added to the reading —

though the chance to interact by commenting or asking questions is either lost or made more formal.

Records and tape-recordings of poetry, read either by actors or by the author, are many, various and well-known in some schools. The local library may have a tapes/records department which you might explore. Recordings cannot replace the immediacy of the live reader, but some do add another dimension which it would be impossible to produce within the classroom; for instance a musical accompaniment – Shakespeare sonnets to a lute background, *Canterbury Tales* to a brass ensemble, modern poetry to jazz. It may be that the recorded reader has a voice more appropriate for the poem than that of the teacher – a woman's voice, for instance, when the poem is clearly from a woman's point of view and the class teacher is a man. Or there may be a marked cultural difference as with Caribbean poetry and only a Caribbean reader can bring out its full effect. Poets are not always the best interpreters of their own work, but as has been said, recordings allow them to speak direct to the class and to supply an additional level of meaning lost to the words written on the page.

Where the recording is accompanied by a film-strip there is an additional stimulus. The visual plays a part in underlining the mood of the poem, or showing the context in which it was written.

Having heard other voices, including the poet's own, reading a poem, pupils might try reading (or preferably re-reading) the poem. After all, the poet hears his or her own voice in the head whilst composing. To imitate or recreate that voice is to come to a closer understanding of the poem through its music. Ted Hughes' northern accent, Robert Frost's dry, almost toneless New England accent, John Betjeman's enthusiasm – each adds a dimension to the meaning of the poem which is not fully evident in the print on the page.

Schools' Broadcasting in radio and television offers a variety of poetry programmes across the age ranges of schooling, from literary commentary on a particular author at the upper end, to a miscellany of jingles, rhymes and short poems on a theme at the lower. The teacher's notes and/or pupil pamphlets which accompany the series are usually very good value for money and contain much material outside the range of usual school anthologies. There are copyright restrictions on the length of time these programmes can be retained if recorded. Teachers' Centres often hold copies of past programmes if you miss one and it is worth checking on just what resources they offer in your area.

Evening television and radio over a period of time can offer a surprising amount of poetry which might be harnessed for use in school hours; not just the epilogue reading with inspiring music, but performances such as the informal *Poems and Pints* programmes; profiles of modern writers like Ted Hughes; documentaries on aspects of modern culture such as Rasta poets and so on. Again it is difficult to replicate this material within the resources of the classroom. Although copyright restrictions mean that playback in school time is not permissible, if the class is strongly recommended to watch or listen at home, it will help to underline that poetry is not just something that belongs in school in English lessons.

5.   Choral speaking

Choral speaking of poetry has suffered a decline in popularity, but working together as a group to produce such a performance involves the close interpretation of a poem and makes it a valuable addition to the range of active learning methods which form an alternative to written comprehension exercises.

The first stage is to select a suitable poem. John Heath-Stubbs' *The History of the Ark* and W.H. Auden's *Night Mail* are well-known examples of substantial poems used for large-scale performance. But almost any poem can be interpreted by the imaginative use of several voices to express contrasts of mood, image and thought. See for instance G.K. Chesterton's *Lepanto* (RB) which encourages use of sound effects:

Dim drums throbbing in the hills half heard

The Gaelic poem *The wicked who would do me harm* (RB) (translated by A. Carmichael) is effective with a humorous treatment, perhaps also with sound effects:

The wicked who would do me harm
May he take the throat disease,
Globularly, spirally, circularly,
Fluxy, pellety, horny-grim.

The approach to a dramatised reading need not always be reverential. Hilaire Belloc's *Matilda* may best be interpreted by a spoof reading – exaggerating the voices, adding disapproving 'tut-tuts' and 'oohs', and using sound effects which add to the humour. Pupils working in groups deciding on how best to read a poem may well see for themselves that the ambiguous ending of Charles Causley's *Timothy Winters* could be brought out by repetition of the last line with a rising intonation.

It is also possible to build up an anthology of poems to be performed around a particular sound effect; for instance, using drums to interpret the various moods of war. Walt Whitman's *Drum Taps* section on the American civil War in *Leaves of Grass* would provide material as well as the better known British war poets. The variety of instruments in the percussion/timpani range is most useful since they give an enormous range of sound effects and yet are fairly easy to play. Even so skill and practice are needed before any serious performance. This is rich ground for co-operation with the music department in a joint production.

The second step towards production is to select the features within the poem which can be highlighted by the music of the human voice – and perhaps by the use of simple percussion, or even of more complex sound effects. The essential features are then explored for possible vocal qualities that can be used and the effect that can be created:

Quality	Range	Effect
volume	loud – soft	angry – soothing
pitch	high – low	tense – relaxed
tone	warm – cold	friendly – forbidding
rhythm	regular – irregular	hypnotic – dramatic
intonation	rising – falling	questioning – answering

The range of considerations for the production includes:
- Contrasting voices – high/low, boy/girl
- Stereophony – placing speakers in different positions in the room
- Antiphony – one voice answering another
- Crescendo/diminuendo – whisper, murmur, shout
- Single or ripple echo of repeated words
- Solo, pair or unison voices.

To exploit the qualities of the voices available for the interpretation of the text, the production team needs imagination as well as knowledge of technique. Clearly it is an advantage to be able to 'hear' an interpretation in the mind's ear and work towards it. At an early stage of working on the script sentences or units of meaning should be broken up, using coloured pens, to make explicit the contrasts implicit in the text. A single word may be given emphasis if within the context it is:
- spoken by a different reader
- spoken by several readers in unison
- given a different cadence
- repeated as an echo (even when the text does not repeat it).

Such artistic licence as suggested in that last point is welcome when it allows pupils to be creative in their interpretations, and to add their own creativity to that of the poet.

With many poems the class themselves will suggest the appropriate approach. If they are shown possible techniques, encouraged to be creative and to work co-operatively, the results can be very rewarding. They can produce genuine interpretations of their own which you will not have thought about. Groups might select their own poems for interpretation, since, if they are involved from the start of the project they are more likely to be committed to it. Transactional talk about how to perform the poem indirectly celebrates its form and meaning.

A reading may also be accompanied by movement. This is perhaps best done outside class time by a group of volunteers, or in collaboration with a specialist movement teacher, since movement calls for special skills and facilities. But it might also be the subject of a drama project or a production bringing together English, Music and Drama staff. Many schools have performed *Oh What a Lovely War* which very flexibly combines music and drama.

A.S.J. Tessimond's *Cats* can serve as a brief example. It is capable of many interpretations, but here we suggest using three high female voices, which complement each other. The interpretation emphasises the hissing in the repeated 's' sounds and the noise of the wind (in line 3). Colour coding could be used on the script to show who speaks which words. Changes of pace are difficult to indicate, but extra stress can be shown by emphasised print or underlining, and loud or soft shown by a stage direction. The interpretation also calls for sound effects – a cymbal stroked with a wire drum stick for instance or a tambourine shaken gently. The first stanza might read as follows:

1+2+3	Cats
2+3	sssssssssssssss
1	no less liquid than their shadows
1	ssssssssssssssssss
3	(*whisper echo*) shadows
2	offer no angles to the wind
	(*cymbal stroked with wire*)
3	they slip (*strike cymbal*)
2	diminished
1	neat
1+2+3	through loopholes
1	less than themselves
2+3	will not be pinned to rules
1+3	or routes for journeys
2	counter
2+3	attack
1	(*very slowly syllable by syllable*)
	with non-res-ist-ance
2	twist (+3)sssssssss
2	enticing
1	through the curving fingers and leave
2	an angered
2+3	empty
1+2+3	fist.

(See Appendix 1b for the complete poem and further suggestions.)

6. Recording

Pupils should also have the opportunity to practise and to hear themselves by using a tape-recorder throughout all stages, from rehearsal to production.

This should be done with some degree of privacy, perhaps in a quiet corner of the classroom, in a stock-room or outside in the corridor if they can be trusted. This will lead to discussion, between themselves and perhaps with the class, followed by revision. A final stage might be a polished reading in the best recording conditions possible, as like a recording studio as can be managed.

If a class has had the opportunity to browse through poetry anthologies, for interest or for a specific purpose, the end-product can be a tape-recorded anthology of the most successful pieces – either the most readable or most appropriate to a theme. The class, working in groups, might be guided by the pattern of some school broadcasts, where an anthology of readings on a theme can have background music and a linking commentary. Good recordings can be catalogued in the school library or resource centre, and should be available to a wider audience. One class can exchange tapes with another in the same school or even in a different one. A programme might be made with a much younger class in mind – perhaps in a feeder junior/middle school. Parents' Evenings, Open Days, School Assembly, a Book Fair are all possible occasions for playback or live performance. Perhaps more importantly, if the school has some form of Listening Centre – even an ear-plug for a cassette tape-recorder – such tapes together with professionally produced records and tapes should be available for private listening. This is appropriate for all levels of ability. In private, the pupil has a chance to muse, imagine and reflect, stopping the tape to recall and re-hear a line in the mind's ear.

6

The sense of sound

Although we think of ours as predominantly a visual age, sound is of particular significance to the poet for two main reasons: one is to do with the way the writer wants us to perceive the world, the other with the way he or she wishes to guide our attention. To expand on the first of these, much of our work in English teaching is related to developing pupils' appreciation of the world around them, not only through the intellect but through their physical senses as well. Sound is one of the ways in which we perceive the world; in our televisual age some may consider it a minor part, but poetry can serve to remind us of how central to our emotions this sense can be, as in Gerard Manley Hopkins' poem *Spring*:

> Thrush
> Through the echoing timber does so rinse and wring
> The ear, it strikes like lightnings to hear him sing.

We, too, as teachers wish to let poetry 'rinse and wring' the senses of our pupils, helping them see the world around them more clearly, not just the new and unknown but also the familiar and commonplace.

Children do have a strong oral tradition of their own which can be used as a bridge with poetry for those who think of it as remote and irrelevant. The youngest pupils of secondary age will still remember playground chants, jokes, rhymes and games. Older pupils will have a more ephemeral sub-culture, drawing on advertising and current slang. But playing with words is common to both ends of the age range.

To explore the world through sound, however, is not to focus solely upon 'beautiful' natural sound, which is so often thought to be 'cissy'. To make the point that poetry can draw our attention to all sound, consider the sound-picture, created in Walt Whitman's poem *Song of Myself*, of below-decks during a sea battle in former times:

> The hiss of the surgeon's knife, the gnawing teeth of his saw,
> wheeze, cluck, swash of falling blood, short wild
> scream, and long dull, tapering groan;

The effects of sound

Poetry can express a cacophony of sound, as in the mediaeval *The Black-smiths* (see Appendix 1a), perhaps the first poem to rail against noise pollution and night-shift working! By contrast, Walter de la Mare's *The Listeners* is famous because it has stillness at its heart, and uses suggestion to create an atmosphere beyond the detail of the heard sounds. In a very different context, William Stafford's *At the bomb testing site* (RB) describes no sound at all, but this silence heightens our awareness of the stillness of the lizard, of the desert and the seemingly endless moment before the colossal noise of the awaited nuclear explosion.

Although poetry is not often used as a vehicle for dialogue, instances where it is can be very evocative. In Wole Soyinka's *Telephone Conversation*, for instance, a black man seeking accommodation is obliged to describe himself over the phone to a potential landlady who, though unheard, is increasingly revealed as prejudiced by the answers to her questions. Robert Browning's dramatic monologues (suitable for older pupils) create character in depth by the subtle nuances of their speech. The exaggerated London East End accent of the tragi-comic *Dahn the Plug'ole* (RB) has wooed many generations of younger poetry classes. In the more recent trans-Atlantic *Saginaw Song* (RB), Theodore Roethke uses the honourable tradition of rumbustious poetry. If we look for it there is a wealth of material available, evoking a range of sound, varied in nature and effect.

The way in which poets use sound to capture and guide our attention is more complicated, because of the many techniques available to the writer and the range of responses of the reader-listener. When language uses sound in a structured way it becomes more memorable. This is particularly significant in a society which relies on the spoken rather than on the written word for passing on much of its literature, its history, its culture. Alliteration, assonance, rhyme, rhythm – these are all mnemonic devices, rooted in the days when the bard or storyteller recited long works such as *The Odyssey* or *Beowulf*. The same techniques have a powerful emotional effect on the listener, serving to soothe or excite, to amuse or sadden. The repeated long vowel sounds in Tennyson's '*Break, Break, Break*' have a doom-laden, mournful effect, reflecting the poem's meaning; whereas Lewis Carroll in *Mad Gardener's Song* (RB) uses rhyme links between such discordant objects as 'fife' and 'wife', or 'chimney piece' and 'husband's niece' for a humorous effect.

Spoken language in a structured form has throughout the ages been enhanced by the accompaniment of music. Poems written for the accompaniment of the lyre are now published for us to read, rather than hear in performance, and much of the original instrumental music is lost. But the tradition of words and music is still very much alive at all levels of sophistication – in pop music, opera, musicals, hymns, satirical songs. We can harness this already familiar and powerful link, taking pupils further in their understanding of both medium and message, if we make them active listeners to the music of the language.

But there is a level beyond the surface structure of poetry, and beyond the emotional response which it evokes. It is the mysterious ingredient x of poetry, to do with meaning which cannot be fully explored or consciously explained. Poetry can be more than the sum of its analysed parts; its meanings can echo inside us, with lines, phrases or images being sounded out inside our heads. It is an idea developed in *The Face of the Horse* by the Russian poet N.A. Zabolotsky (translated by D. Weissbort) from which the title of this book is taken:

> And if a man should see
> The horse's magical face
> He would tear out his own impotent tongue
> And give it to the horse. For
> This magical creature is surely worthy of it.
> Then we should hear words.
> Words large as apples. Thick
> As honey or buttermilk.
> Words which penetrate like flame
> And, once within the soul, like fire in some hut,
> Illuminate its wretched trappings,
> Words which do not die
> And which we celebrate in song.

We should be aware as teachers that the poem may be killed by too many words of commentary; that its sound may only be appreciated fully by contrast with some kind of silence. This may be provided immediately after a reading so that all can recollect their thoughts; or there may be no discussion of the poem at all, with pupils being allowed to take their books home, where some at least may re-read, and others may think beyond the poem. To help develop this confidence with poetry, there are many ways of encouraging pupils to appreciate the sound of poetry more fully.

Starting points

With a new class it is a good idea to find out what they already know, and rather than risk a direct question which could produce groans ('What poetry have you done before?') it is better to focus more specifically on some particular aspect which they can recall from previous work, either individually or in groups, or can investigate through research outside school. There are four areas, in particular, which offer rich material for starting work on the sound of poetry.

Firstly, there is the poetry all around us, in the world outside the classroom. Women's magazines, teenage magazines, local press, songs of all kinds, advertisements on radio, T.V., cinema, hoardings and buses, popular entertainers on the media, dialect songs – all can provide examples of poetry of one kind or another which appeal to the ear. The class may have in it a keen musician who has copies of sheet music or have magazines containing current song lyrics which could be looked at in class. Morning assembly hymns are also a possible source – the Victorians had a taste for emotionally charged images helped along by sonorous verse and equally sonorous music.

Secondly, people can be a useful resource: parents, neighbours, relatives across the generations can be asked what poetry they remember, and whether they can quote any lines. Examples can be recorded – either on tape or through written notes, and then brought back to the classroom to share with others and discuss. The class can build up a collection in a folder, on tape or as a wall display. The purpose of this kind of work is to explore the oral tradition; hence, enquiry might include proverbs and sayings if formal poetry draws a blank. In a small way, such enquiry might help to keep oral tradition alive, since pupils will be talking to an older generation in what is probably a different way about material which is infrequently discussed explicitly. In a multi-cultural school the sharing of information of this kind can be fascinating; other cultures can be far more rich than one's own in their oral tradition and far more active currently in creating new 'popular' poetry. Sharing in the classroom though requires a sympathetic audience, patience and even a translation in some instances.

Thirdly, there is the oral culture of young children – playground games, skipping chants, insults. *The Lore and Language of School-children* by I. and P. Opie (Oxford University Press, 1959) is still a classic study and could be used to give the class examples of what is meant. Much of this material uses strong rhymes and half-rhymes, which can be pointed out when examples are reported back. Further work can involve nursery rhymes, riddles and folk sayings, many of which have interesting interpretations – *Ring a roses*, for example, with its possible reference to the Great Plague, and *Humpty Dumpty* as a reference to a siege machine in the Civil War. They are interesting because rhythm and rhyme are used not only to give shape but also to celebrate ritual. 'Here comes the chopper to chop off your head,' addresses Death through ritualistic formula. Aphorisms such as, 'A stitch in time saves nine', trim down experience to the bare essentials.

In all kinds of enquiry work, pupils may achieve the most positive results if they are given a specific task. A checklist of items to look for and a format for recording the information is one way of guiding their efforts:

Checklist

Rhymes – nursery / skipping / insult
Riddles
Proverbs

Aphorisms

Jingles

Lyrics – pop and rock / other songs / hymns

Poems – humorous / serious / nature/etcetera.

Record sheet

Name ....   *Class* ....

Quotation

Where you heard it

Who said it

Type of poem

Finally, the class's own experience of poetry, at any age and stage, is a resource in itself. They may, however, have developed an apathy towards poetry, or regard it as a private medium, in which case if you ask them to express a view publicly it will need to be handled with care. If you ask in the first instance for a written response from an individual rather than an oral one from the whole class there is less chance of a hostile reaction growing up in the class as a whole. Then, if you ask for the writing to be only a jotted note of a first line, a title, a catch-phrase, a sketch of content – whatever they can remember – of a particular kind of poetry, they have a specific task which again is more likely to succeed than a general exhortation to remember 'poetry you have liked'. Tasks might relate to a topic or a theme or a genre – for example, animals, the sea, the weather, nursery rhymes, etc. You can share in such research, chatting with previous class teachers and prompting the class's memory. Remembering can become a competitive game and might be an enjoyable starting point.

1.   Collections

Poems

After you have established a convention of collecting over a period of time snippets of poetry from an oral tradition, the class can make a collection of published poems which focus on sound – either complete poems or shorter quotations. This collection might contain explicit references to the sense of sound in life or examples where the sound of the poem itself excites attention – or of course both. If such a collection can be 'published' in a folder or recorded as a cassette tape – always available for people to add to or browse in at will – this will serve the purpose of promoting active interest. Pop songs, football chants, sub-culture slogans can find a place here, particularly if they are the key to motivating those who would otherwise be completely alienated by the usual anthology material.

For further work on the structure of poetry, the collection might be presented in a format which highlights the particular feature of aural interest. Sounds could be underlined in different colours – red for onomatopoeia, blue for alliteration and so on.

Examples collected might range from the simple to the complex – and even of notorious howlers which have the wrong effect. (Gerard Manley Hopkins could be a candidate with his rhyming of 'communion' with 'boon he on' in the poem *A bugler's first communion*.) Further levels of sophistication can be added with more advanced pupils who might collect examples of half-rhyme or assonance (see Appendix 2 for explanation of literary terms).

Words

Further research might be aimed at the study of individual words, for their own sake and for the music that is in them. Focus might be on newly coined words; old words which have changed their meaning, perhaps using Dr. Johnson's Dictionary; dialect words, using the resources of the class and people it knows together with a dialect dictionary; word parallels, using a thesaurus. A thesaurus is a particularly useful tool because it gives pupils access to a greatly extended vocabulary and in their own writing they can, if they know the meaning which they wish to convey, select words which fit the sound pattern of their poem more closely. An increased range of choices not only opens up subtler shades of meaning, it allows pupils to give their thought greater harmony through more skilful working of the form.

Similarly a rhyming dictionary, probably a rare object in schools, extends the range of possibilities for the young writer. Some might argue that it encourages a lazy attitude to writing, but that need not be the case. With such a resource available, pupils' writing should be more expressive than before because the potentially tyrannical effect of rhyme on meaning is reduced. It is up to the teacher to see that the use of such tools does not encourage laziness.

2.   Sound patterns

Both traditional nursery rhymes and children's own lore are rich in sound patterns, and younger classes will be able to relate back to this early stage in their lives. Older pupils may have a resistance to what they see as childish, but throughout the English curriculum they are likely to have encountered a wide range of models of poetry. This past experience is a useful resource which can be called upon when they are ready for more explicit teaching of the patterns of poetry. Models which they will be familiar with, such as limericks, will demonstrate a pattern strong enough to be heard. This kind of teaching, where implicit knowledge is raised to the level of consciousness, is taught most positively in parallel with pupils' own writing (see Chapter 9).

    1.   **Alliteration:** This is a kind of 'front-rhyme' in that the beginnings of words are linked by the same sound, whereas what we call 'rhyme' is an 'end-rhyme', the link being between the endings of words. Alliteration was the major structural device used by Anglo-Saxon poetry, and the Middle

English *Sir Gawain and the Green Knight* carried on the tradition. *The Blacksmiths* (see Appendix 1a) is a mediaeval example, and the technique is still strong in Welsh poetry. Dylan Thomas used a great deal of alliteration, together with the associated internal sound pattern of *assonance*. The opening passage of his *Under Milk Wood* is well known for its use of sound patterns to build up a sense impression of a particular time and place. Going back in time in pupils' experience, Edward Lear's *An Animal Alphabet* (RB) uses alliteration alone as the structural device. In modern idiom, alliteration is a form of patterning frequent in newspaper headlines and advertising slogans, and hence one that pupils will be very familiar with.

2. **Free verse:** This is a misnomer since this kind of verse usually does have some form, and sound is one means of giving a poetic shape to the writing. Take for instance D.H. Lawrence's *Man and Bat* (RB) which uses the drama of sound to catch the reader or listener's attention: 'My room, a crash-box over that great stone rattle / The Via de' Bardi...' Or W.H. Auden's version of the Old English poem *The Wanderer* which begins with the strongly alliterative line, 'Doom is dark and deeper than any sea dingle'. If pupils encounter such poems as these frequently then the structure behind 'free verse' becomes more apparent, and the deceptive ease of verse like Frank O'Hara's *A true account of talking to the sun at Fire Island* (RB) can be fully appreciated.

3. **Onomatopoeia:** This is a device which has appeal to young children, and which secondary school pupils are likely to have had experience of in their reading and writing at primary level (whether or not they can spell it!). Because of its importance in poetry as a dramatic effect it deserves continued focus throughout the secondary school. Lewis Carroll's *Jabberwocky* could be used with younger pupils as an example of the suggestiveness possible in sound alone:

> One, two! One, two! And through and through
> The vorpal blade went snicker-snack!
> He left it dead, and with its head
> He went galumphing back.

That is a good starting point for developing pupils' critical ability; from appreciating playing with sound through to a serious awareness of how sound can evoke wider feelings and hence deeper meanings. Consider Carl Sandburg's *Jazz Fantasia* where the evocation of the sounds made by the instruments also creates the moods of the musicians and of the listener:

> Moan like an autumn wind high in the lonesome treetops,
>   moan soft like
> you wanted somebody terrible, cry like a racing car slipping
>   away from a
> motorcycle cop, bang-bang!

Or Wilfred Owen's *Anthem for Doomed Youth* which is a vivid sound picture of trench warfare:

> What passing-bells for these who die as cattle?
> Only the monstrous anger of the guns.
> Only the stuttering rifles' rapid rattle
> Can patter out their hasty orisons.

4.   **Repetition:** One of the simplest sound devices in poetry is the repetition of a word or phrase in a particular pattern – most obviously, at the start of a line or as a refrain at the end of each verse. The song, 'These are a few of my favourite things', is a list of items held together only by the general concept of the title and a simple rhyme scheme. You might know Edgar Allen Poe's *Bells*, which, with the repetition of the word 'bells' at least ten times in each stanza, takes this device to its extreme. Laura Riding's *Children*, part of *Forgotten Girlhood* (RB), belies a simple structure with a repeated refrain, 'Come back early or never come', which becomes increasingly mysterious.

5.   **Rhyme:** Sound patterns in poetry can have a powerful mnemonic quality – invaluable in pre-literate times when a society's culture could only be handed on to succeeding generations by means of a bard's memory. Rhyme is such a strong form of patterning that for many children it becomes an essential part of their concept of poetry. Their earliest experience of poetry will have been nursery rhymes, with their strongly stressed rhythm and rhyme schemes – 'Little Jack Horner sat in a corner', or 'Doctor Foster went to Gloucester', and so on. In the early stages of writing poetry, this strongly held impression can be a disadvantage, as sense is often sacrificed for the sake of rhyme. The pupil's linguistic resources are severely stretched to supply more than a brief sequence of words with both the desired meaning and the desired rhyme. There is no virtue in banning rhyme until they are 'old enough to handle it'; pupils will learn through experiment and improve with practice.

To reduce the conflict between rhyming pattern and meaning, it is worth looking at nonsense verse or bad rhymes for the sake of their humour; free verse is another possibility, where rhyme might not be used at all, except as a special dramatic effect. It is clearly best to work with short poems, because the rhyming requirement is reduced – not to mention the virtue of clarity in perception and expression which brevity encourages. In longer poems we can expect only occasional rhymes, which work well in partnership with meaning. Some forms are more tolerant; for instance the traditional broadsheet ballad allows for the rhyme (i.e. line endings) to depend on words which were clichés or of lesser importance, and this is an enabling device for young writers.

The technique of *half-rhyme* opens up more creative opportunities since the sound connection is less exact, allowing the writer a wider choice of

words to express the desired meaning. At senior level Elizabeth Jennings'
poem *The Enemies* (see Appendix 1a) could be used as a model, with
half-rhymes of 'filled' / 'told' / 'field' in the second stanza, and 'friends' /
'hands' / 'minds' in the third. The half-rhymes add to the melancholy effect
of the poem, as the shifting relationships of sounds reflect the strained
interactions of people in the invaded town.

6.   **Rhythm:** Traditionally rhythm was described using technical terminology devised by critics of classical verse; dactyl, iamb, spondee,
trochee, and so on. The terminology relates to syllabic length and hence to
the stress pattern of the words in each line of the poem. The description
then extends to the overall length of the poem's standard line. The
Shakespearean 'iambic pentameter' is perhaps the metrical pattern most
frequently referred to now using this classical terminology. This is partly
because Shakespeare is so widely taught, but also because the iambic stress
pattern (two syllables, the second stressed) is one of the patterns which
best fits the natural stress patterns of English, and hence is used for a great
deal of poetry.

Alexander Pope's *Essay on Criticism* includes clever examples of
classical stress patterns, while passing comment on their effect.

> A needless Alexandrine ends the song
> That like a wounded snake drags its slow length along.

Writers educated in the classical tradition continued to write according to
such regular, determined patterns long after the classical age of the
eighteenth century. Thomas Hardy's 'Woman much missed how you call
to me, call to me', for instance, uses regular dactyls (one long stressed
syllable followed by two short unstressed ones).

However, traditional metre had also to take account of natural stress
required by the meaning – how a speaker would naturally emphasise
certain words to bring out the intended meaning, with the appropriate
tone, intonation, pitch and so on. There are usually fewer stresses per line
than the metre suggests, and to read exactly according to the stress pattern
makes a poem sound forced, as if it were being read by a robot. To analyse
the complex patterns of metrical and natural stress as they coincide or
conflict within a poem is an advanced activity; and sensitive appreciation
of the sound of poetry certainly does not depend on such ability.
Consequently, recent approaches to teaching poetry have moved away
from technical analysis. This is not just a question of changing taste; it is
that technical analysis is no longer so appropriate. The metrical patterns of
the classics were best suited to a multi-syllabic language such as Latin, but
English, which favours shorter words, can be fitted to Latinate patterns
only with considerable difficulty. Less regular patterns are now more
predominant, so that classical terminology fits much of the modern poetry
studied in schools less exactly. One of the most famous examples of

rhythm in traditional anthologies must be W.H. Auden's *Night Mail,* in which the patterns of rhythm change to suggest the changing tempo of a journey by steam-train. Even this has become a piece of history as our culture has changed, with such sounds and rhythms made obsolete with the coming of welded track and electric trains. But there should be no sense of loss; Pope, Hardy and Auden are still available to us, and the canon expands to include new rhythms, like those of the Caribbean, for instance. James Berry's *In-a Brixtan Markit* (see Appendix 1a) has a powerfully flexible rhythm which follows the drama of the scene rather than a pre-set metrical pattern. Use of the Oliver Bernard technique (see chapter 10) will show the range of stress patterns which different readers can select from to bring out their interpretation of a poem's meaning.

Further information on sound patterns is given in the *Glossary of Technical Terms* (Appendix 2). For the majority of pupils the most direct way into understanding sound effects will be through active interpretation of poetry using dramatic reading. This will bring to life not only the traditional patterns outlined above, but also the other more subtle patterns of intonation, pace, pitch and tone, all of which contribute to and comment on the meaning of the poem.

3.   Links with music

In both poetry and music, tastes and techniques change. Usually we teach poetry from anthologies as if it were dateless; we do not make great play with the changes in values, customs and beliefs which have taken place since the time of writing. An appealing way of making a historical study more interesting is to investigate song lyrics and music as a 'Then and Now' theme.

Old records and sheet music are suitable data to work with; poetry of the same period is then brought in as the second stage, to build up a broader picture of a period such as the Victorian age – Tennyson's 'Come in to the garden, Maud', for instance, leading into a wider study of poetry of the period. The satire of W.S. Gilbert, too, deserves to be taken out of the context of the annual school Gilbert & Sullivan production for closer study. Satirical songs could be a separate project, taking material from across a wide span of time and society. Music hall songs of the 1900s are a rich resource as well, playing on a wide range of emotional effects – pathos, humour, the sensational and the macabre. First World War soldiers often had their own versions of patriotic songs; these could be linked with the war poets and their transition from Georgian attitudes. (The stage play and film *Oh What a Lovely War* used such material.) Then there is the Jazz Age of the twenties and thirties with its heady mood of social freedom – a high point in witty musicals – followed by the blues of the Depression. Next there are the nostalgia songs of the Second World War such as 'The White Cliffs of Dover' and the witty, brittle lyrics of Noel Coward. Several early rock songs by the Beatles have become established classroom material (*When I'm sixty-four* and *She's leaving home*), as have protest songs of the sixties by such writers as Bob Dylan. As for the current music scene, the children are the experts in that, as ever, and will know which music papers to buy for copies of the lyrics.

Sound is a dynamic force in poetry and cries out to be heard – whether silently in the inner ear of the reader or aloud through performance. The approaches outlined in this chapter concentrate more upon using the inner ear to increase the sensitivity of pupils' appreciation. In the next chapter, on drama, we concentrate on interpreting poetry through active participation in performance.

7

Drama

There is much about the essence of poetry which is dramatic: the exploration of tensions and conflicts, the probing of relationships between people and the world. But there is an essential difference between drama and poetry as media for exploring and expressing experience. The ballet dancer Nijinsky was once asked by an admirer to explain the meaning of one of his dances. He is said to have replied, 'If I could tell you that, why should I dance it?' We must respect the distinctive qualities of art forms; they lose their meaning in translation.

One of the significant differences between poetry and drama is their treatment of time. Most drama explores relationships in an extended time sequence, with reference to real time, usually through the chronology of narrative. Only some poetry – particularly the ballad – relates in this way to time and narrative events. It is far more common for poetry to relate to a snapshot of time, a brilliant flash of perception. Another distinction is that drama is usually about taking part, interacting, enacting, whereas poetry is more frequently about observing and commenting on the inner reality of people, places and experiences rather than explicit actions.

For these fundamental reasons, it is unlikely that all poems can be translated into dramatic activity. Sometimes, however, the meaning of a poem can be explored obliquely through drama; and such an exploration of the meaning of poetry need not be confined to only the most dramatic of poems, nor be a literal translation of a poem into explanatory or expansive action.

There are three powerful justifications for using drama to explore poetry. Firstly, workshop activities extend the time over which students are involved with each particular poem; this increases absorption time. We can easily underestimate the density of language, experience and allusion in poetry and allow too little time for it to make its impact, for pupils to absorb it and build upon it. They will spend a far greater length of time in contact with the central ideas of a poem when involved in working out a practical response in drama. Secondly, there is the advantage of direct pupil involvement in practical activity and problem-solving. If poetry is a dense medium in both its concepts and its language, it will seem highly abstract to adolescents. Physical involvement with ideas is likely to involve them more successfully than more cerebral approaches alone. Thirdly, and most important, by enacting the experience they project their whole selves into it. In the process, not just the head but the heart will be involved as their experience of the world is extended and shaped. Although Piaget's theory of cognitive development suggests that children pass through a stage of concrete operations in the primary school, clearly adults retain the ability to learn through practical involvement, and for many people of all ages it is the most effective way to learn. It will still be appropriate to use drama as a practical and engaging way of exploring set texts in all genres throughout schooling up to advanced level.

The range of possible approaches is wide, and will often be suggested by particular poems. But in broad terms it is possible to distinguish three distinct positions on a continuum:

1. **Exploration:** where the central idea or ideas of the poem act as a springboard. Pupils use the idea to move away from the poem itself in order to explore related concepts through drama activities.
2. **Improvisation:** where the focus stays within the poem in order to tease out and expand its dense allusions through improvised drama without final shaping into a performance.
3. **Performance:** where the poem provides a clear structure for a drama script, and there is a notion of theatrical performance, with an audience.

The movement in these three approaches is from a divergent exploration of ideas expressed in a poem to focused interpretation of a poem as a 'script'.

Exploration

Drama can be used to give focus to an open-ended exploration of the concepts within a chosen poem. It can be applied to a very large range of poems, including those which are dense in meaning, and perhaps have a general rather than specific range of reference. Such poems need not have the dramatic ingredients of character interaction, dialogue, or story-line, since the aim is not to interpret or translate the poem line by line. Often the drama experience will be brief. It will be just sufficient to identify the main idea or ideas in the poem in order to focus on exploring the pupils' experience of these in the world. This literature/life linkage makes the 'exploration' approach useful as a warm-up before either improvisation or performance. For instance, deeper insight into an aspect of villagers' roles in the improvisation of *The Dam* and *The Enemies* described below might come from a warm-up which explores an aspect of family life, such as the lack of communication at the centre of a poem such as Alasdair Maclean's *Among Ourselves* (T):

> Among ourselves we rarely speak.
> Our tongues are thick with custom.

Or the viewpoint of old people using the poem *Old Men* by Tony Connor.

These poems might also provide a way into exploring Ralph McTell's gently accusatory song-ballad *Streets of London*, with its descriptions of the old, the homeless, the 'down and out' people in a capital city.

A poem might provide the springboard for a longer project, on a topic like 'The Circus' for instance, using such poems as James Kirkup's *The Equilibrist* (T) or Louis Macneice's *Trapezists* (T):

> Intricacy of engines,
> Delicacy of darkness;
> They rise into the tent's
> Top like deep-sea divers ...

Since there are a lot of poems about circuses and the various circus performers, including animals, this could be a challenging target for an anthology of poems, perhaps setting pupils the task of finding more poems around the theme before and during the drama series. Again, the starting point is in selecting roles, trying out mime, building up a sequence of actions, developing dialogue where that is called for; and, in between, brainstorming, discussing and evaluating in pairs or groups, or with the whole class, the teacher acting as consultant, adviser, provocateur – but problem-solver only where necessary.

A series about 'Space', for instance, might be provoked by the lyrics of David Bowie's pop song *Space Odyssey* using the conversation between ground control and Major Tom. This can be linked to Edwin Morgan's *Spacepoem 3: Off course*:

> the golden flood   the weightless seat
> the cabin song   the pitch black

Some poems stand alone though to provoke exploration through drama, they are so dense in emotional meaning. For example Miles Gibson's *Jump* (T):

> She stands
> on the thin black line
> of the window ledge
>
> and implores that the wind
> should blow out her life ...

What has brought this about? What can we say to the girl to make her want to go on living? These are among the many questions provoked by the poem, and are what the drama would focus on to explore the range of possible answers. Just how to organise the drama and what techniques to use, is for the teacher to decide, in conjunction with the pupils. But the precise details of technique are less important than that pupils should actively take part in exploring the central concepts of the poem, and make those concepts their own. They are being asked to use their experiential knowledge of the world and sometimes to conjecture what might happen to others or to themselves. That is the underlying theme of this chapter and the most important justification for using drama to engage with poetry.

Improvisation

The focus here is not on performance. Improvisation might lead on to a performance but the resulting script would not be the original poem but an adaptation. This approach, therefore, is applicable to poems which are not completely dramatic in themselves – although they might contain one or other of the necessary ingredients: an implicit story-line, an explicit context or a cast of more than one person to allow for dramatic interaction.

Ballads can be usefully approached in this way since their narrative form makes them amenable to development into story drama. *The Penguin Book of Ballads* contains many suitable examples. *The Buffalo Skinners*, for instance, describes episodes in the lives of buffalo hunters in the American West. The episodic structure allows for syndication – where groups in the class each take on an episode to develop, and the combined effort of all the group produces a complete story drama. There are many possible approaches, and the class should be free to develop their own ideas, since the aim is essentially exploratory. Available techniques, though, would include the use of a narrator to link the episodes, naturalistic dialogue based on the events suggested in the poem, or mimed action to a choral reading.

There are several ballads about Robin Hood and his deeds which could provide episodes for an extended drama, covering his life from the forming of his band to his death. By contrast *The Gresford Disaster* about a coal-mining accident is brief, but gives the basis for an exploration of conditions underground. Similarly *The Greenland Whale* could be the basis for a documentary drama about whaling, perhaps linked with whaling songs and shanties along the lines of the stage play *Oh What a Lovely War* which used soldiers' songs to explore themes of the First World War.

Another group of poems which benefit from the 'improvisation' approach are ones which centre on a village or similar complete community, since they allow the whole class to take part in one event without the need for syndication. This fosters co-operation within the larger group. It is not necessarily more difficult for the teacher to handle, though it is important in the first stage to make sure everyone in the class has a positive role to play. If for instance the poem is set in the past, it would not be appropriate for a pupil to decide his or her role is to mend video-recorders. The sequence should begin with a discussion of the possibilities appropriate to the time and place of the poem; then let pupils choose the role they feel most comfortable with. That way they are opting into the activity, not following orders mindlessly; each person is then more likely to bring personal experience to bear, and explore what seems personally relevant, in relation to the poem.

Patrick Dickinson's *The Dam* (TWF) describes the coming of a reservoir to flood a village: how at first the people were glad of the work, at the time of the depression, but afterwards regretted the loss.

> This was our valley, yes.
> Our valley till they came
> And chose to build the dam.
> All the village worked on it
> And we were lucky of course
> All through the slump we had
> Good jobs; they were too well paid
> For the water rose ninety feet.
> And covered our houses; yes – ...

The situation has a lot of potential for drama because of the conflicts involved. Some of the people in the village must have opposed the scheme when it was first suggested. Perhaps some resisted all the way through. The village as a context offers a lot of varied roles to explore: shopkeeper, schoolteacher, religious leader, rich and poor; and various groupings: family, friends, work colleagues, societies.

The first stage is to set up the village in the drama space, each person taking on the role which most appeals: within the family first of all – father, mother, child – then by their role in work or in the society. There is no need for scenery or staging, just the demarcation of an area to serve as house and garden for each group, and then places outside where they might meet – the village green, shops, the church. It need not be set in the class's own society, and there might be very different settings, such as a bazaar, and a mosque. But if it is to pick up the hints in the poem of the Depression in England in the 1930s, it might be helpful to discuss the conditions of the time, perhaps using well-illustrated reference, and then to ensure that not all the groups are wealthy farmers.

The second stage of the drama then is to develop interaction, within the family, as part of a normal day, using mimed action but with as much speech as is wanted. The teacher's role here is to circulate among the groups, asking questions to focus their attention, making suggestions unobtrusively. It is possible to ask groups to demonstrate particular actions for the class, but this is unnecessary if your priority is to get them involved in the meaning of the poem rather than in the techniques of acting.

The third stage is to call a meeting to announce to the villagers that the building of a dam is proposed and that their village will be flooded. The teacher can act in many roles throughout any drama, and here the role of spokesperson for the water company, an outsider to the village, would best be taken by the teacher. As spokesperson the teacher can introduce information about conditions as they were at the time and clarify the conflicting issues. Later the teacher may change role, and come in as a newspaper reporter, perhaps, or an agent provocateur such as a dispossessed farmer to sharpen up one side of the conflict. Other roles might be that of site engineer, foreman of the gang sent to pull down the first house, police sergeant – but not the ultimate decision-maker. The aim is always to force an issue for the pupils but for them to decide the solution.

One way to heighten the tension is to have only some of the villagers taken on as workers on the dam, the others continuing with their previous roles. Then the villagers have to ask what is going on: they might be in the way and be asked to move; they might have less money than the workers, and so on. Finally, however, the group is reunited when the reservoir is filled and they are all 'dispossessed'.

During this slow build-up of the drama it is possible to go back to earlier parts in the narrative to repeat them for confidence building, or to adapt and develop ideas. It might also be possible to develop a written script, since the words people say will be of significance within this language-oriented activity.

So the stages will develop, following a process of discussion, rehearsal, replay, evaluation, with the teacher moving in and out of role as suits the development best.

The Enemies by Elizabeth Jennings (T) is another poem with a village setting, but is more complex in meaning, with its metaphoric significance, and is therefore more suitable for older pupils. It is set in a village in an unspecified time and place, which allows the group first of all to negotiate in discussion which context they would feel most at home in. (The poem is reprinted in full in Appendix 1a.)

The next decision is whether to divide the class into two, with a large group as the villagers, and a smaller group as the invaders. The advantage of having the invaders imagined and not real is that the poem itself has a mystical quality and speaks of 'minds I used to walk in'. Younger students, though, are likely to want a real presence to work against, and as long as it is made clear that there is to be no physical conflict, then there should be no difficulty in having a group of invaders.

The two groups should work out their characteristic actions, and the teacher's leading questions can prompt this. For the villagers: what are their roles, who are their friends, what do they do during the day, where is their house and how is it set up? For the invaders: how do they act, are they soldiers, who are their leaders, how do they speak, what is their real purpose there? A strong degree of secrecy about this group's decisions will add a great deal to the atmosphere of the drama. The poem has a chronology to be followed, and building on that, the stages of the drama are:

1. The villagers acting normally at the end of the day.
2. The invaders arriving, being shown in and entertained – perhaps being shown around the houses and the villagers' possessions. One invader to each household could be the ratio.
3. The next morning the villagers meet outside in the street to exchange views, observations, anecdotes of what happened.
4. The appearance of the invaders could be introduced; perhaps coming down to breakfast in their 'guest' house, then going out into the street.
5. Finally the villagers go about their business for the day, but with a sharp contrast in attitude towards each other compared with the previous evening, the first stage.

Other poems which might be added here are *The Little Cart* by Ch'En Tzu-Lung (T) describing the flight of refugees, which might lead on to the evacuation of the village; or *Conquerors* by Henry Treece which is about the feelings of despair among soldiers when they see the ravaged village they are supposed to have conquered. (The poem is reprinted in full in Appendix 1a.) That might lead to the departure of the invaders.

The final outcome will always be unpredictable, and that is the excitement and challenge of drama. Pupils are genuinely co-operating in re-creating experience and in finding out about themselves and about the meanings of literature in genuinely novel ways.

Performance

In the preparation of a poem for performance there is a continuum of theatricality from solo dramatic reading, through group choral speaking (see Chapter 5), on to formal verse drama like T.S. Eliot's *Murder in the Cathedral*. For our purposes published poetic drama is less significant in classroom work than the more informal middle ground of poetry, which can be celebrated more intensely through performance before an audience of some kind.

1. Live or recorded?

The advantage of working towards a performance in school is the high motivation and concentration produced when a group wants to impress an audience. But it is not usually a straightforward matter to set up an audience as and when required. Another class in the school, or a class from a local primary school would be the closest to hand, but that still requires special arrangements. A very rewarding substitute for a live audience is a simple video camera. The recording can be shown to any audience at any future date, but there is the added advantage that the group performing can also see, appreciate and analyse themselves, which in turn increases motivation.

It widens the range of practical poetry activities if one group takes charge of the filming and feeds its observations into the various stages of discussion and rehearsal. There would need to be a camera operator, but the crew could be expanded to the larger team of:

- *floor manager* – to quieten the 'studio', make sure everyone is in their place, to act as link between camera operator and 'studio'.
- *video-recordist* – to make sure that the recorder actually operates, and is started from the right place every time, for recording and playback.
- *assistant camera operator* – to help the camera operator decide on, then remember the sequence of shots.
- *sound-recordist* – to set up the microphone, perhaps moving it nearer to particular voices during the recording.

Usually the audience will be the remainder of the class, divided into groups for workshop activity, who will watch each other's interpretations. After any performance a range of responses is possible from those who took part and those who watched. It can be very helpful to the class if they are told beforehand what might be most appropriate. One of the least obvious but often most appropriate responses is silence, to give time for all to reflect and absorb the experience. Applause might be most appropriate, no matter whether the mood of the piece be solemn or light. Those who take part usually need reassurance about how they did and applause supplies this immediate feedback.

Either silence or applause might be followed by free or focused discussion. Free discussion can begin with an open invitation to share personal reactions, though it is best to encourage a positive response, with a question like, 'What did you enjoy most about the performance?', or the more neutral, 'What caught your attention?' Focused discussion will relate to aspects of the performance as an interpretation of the poem. It will increase their involvement, self-confidence and critical awareness if the performers themselves lead this discussion, asking the audience which of their ideas worked best, and answering questions on why they chose to interpret the poem as they did.

2. Mime interpretation

The anonymous mediaeval poem *The Blacksmiths* (see Appendix 1a for full text) does not have a strong narrative structure, and so would be difficult to develop into a performance drama directly, but it does describe a particular scene very clearly. This kind of poetry particularly suits the technique of mimed action as an interpretation to accompany a dramatic reading. The poem concerns blacksmiths working in a forge and younger pupils, in particular, could explore that vivid context using appropriate movements, and synchronising their mime with a reading of the poem in the background.

A class of 30 children would be divided into six groups of five. One group would prepare a dramatic reading, taking account of the techniques described in Chapter 5, whilst the other five groups discuss possible action sequences of work in a forge: shoeing horses, beating out wrought iron, pouring molten metal. All need to work as part of a team: one pumps the bellows, one fetches coal or water on command, two strike with hammers, and so on.

The group preparing the reading looks carefully at the text and decides how to bring it to life. They decide which voices will read which words, phrases or lines; what should be the volume, tone and pitch; what is to be solo, pair or unison. They might decide that they want actors in the groups to speak some of the words such as 'Lus, bus' or 'Tik, tak' at the right moment, either echoing the reading group or taking over the reading temporarily. There is really no end to the variations possible, and to the creative ingenuity which pupils can show in solving the challenge of bringing a script to life.

During the exploration phase the teacher's role is to circulate among the groups, where possible listening and advising, rather than giving orders, to allow pupils to generate their own responses as far as possible. After this period of individual group discussion and experiment there come the rehearsal stages, necessary for a smooth sequence of actions to be developed and then to be synchronised with the reading. At the first rehearsal stage, groups decide on roles and try out their parts, commenting freely to each other as they put together a sequence. There will be little co-ordination between the groups at this stage, but this will be followed by a general discussion when all can contribute opinions on how the drama could be developed.

At the second rehearsal stage, the reading group gives the others a sense of the time available for their mime sequence by simply reading through the poem whilst the groups perform their actions as best they can. The whole class then discusses again what went well, what they could expand and what omit.

At the third rehearsal stage, the groups polish their roles, and perhaps add sound effects to complement the sounds in the poem. Clearly there is the opportunity for some to take advantage here and this stage could be missed out – though that would be a pity since mime alone does not completely capture the energy of the poem. If the group is learning to co-operate, is allowed to make decisions as to how the piece is performed and is free to comment constructively on how it is developing, then individuals are less likely to misbehave.

So the process of rehearsal moves on from group work to whole-group performance, increasing in effectiveness at each stage. At any stage, before or after, or during a break in the rehearsals, it might add extra interest to show colour pictures or play sound effects tapes about working with metal, or to read a poem such as Seamus Heaney's *The Forge*. This is a difficult poem for younger pupils, but the strong context of the drama work could allow them to grasp what would otherwise be beyond them.

The final performance might be a part of a miscellany production mounted on the school stage or it could be recorded with a video camera, which this approach suits well.

3. Readers' theatre

In the U.S.A. and Canada there is an approach to interpretation known as 'Readers' Theatre' which is a development from choral speaking and mime-accompanied reading. It adds simple movement and gesture to a reading without going so far as full dramatisation. Readers interact and respond to each other with facial expression, gesture and movement, in some cases moving around as if on a stage. It calls for stylised rather than natural movement as in mime, which may seem demanding, but because the script is retained and is not learned by heart, it is a useful approach for a semi-formal production without the weeks of rehearsal that the use of a memorised script requires.

For example, to choreograph the movement in Tessimond's *Cats* for a Readers' Theatre production you would want to emphasise significant words in this way:

hand movement	*twist, fist, skinned*
facial expression	*skinned, flatter*
body movement	*liquid, slip, obsequious, flatter*
moving around the others	*angles, shadows, routes, attack, retire-return, answer*

Henry Treece's *Conquerors* could be interpreted with more naturalistic movement, perhaps with the poem read by a narrator and the mimed action of a group in the background. However the tradition of Readers' Theatre would suggest a closer and more symbolic relationship between the participants, who would perform in a line facing the audience. They would suggest the presence of objects referred to by looking or turning to 'see' them in pre-arranged parts of the room. They would suggest action and movement by use of the arms and upper body. Facial expression would suggest emotion. They can interact with each other, and the action is not restricted just to the person speaking at a particular time. You have to see the effect to realise the power of the technique, which comes from the close focus of the audience's attention on small symbols and evocative suggestion rather than on the larger-scale effects of full dramatisation. The following is how a Readers' Theatre interpretation of Henry Treece's poem might look:

> (*All readers walk in slowly in a line, suggesting weariness – not too caricatured or it looks ludicrous!* SOLDIERS *are numbered 1–4 from stage left to right.* NARRATOR *enters last and stays slightly apart from the others. All turn to face audience in a line as* NARRATOR *begins.*)

NARRATOR   By sundown we came to a hidden village where all the air was still – and

SOLDIER 1   No sound met our tired ears

SOLDIER 2   Save for the sorry drip of rain from blackened trees.

> *(Pause for movement – each does something slightly differ-
> ent: pulling up collar, hugging self into coat, looking up at
> rain, pulling down a hat, wiping wet off forehead.)*

NARRATOR   And the melancholy song of swinging gates.

SOLDIER 3   *(slowly and peering into audience)* Then through a broken
pane *(pause, as if just making it out)* some of us saw

SOLDIER 4   A dead bird in a rusting cage

SOLDIER 3   Still pressing his thin tattered breast against the bars

SOLDIER 4   His beak wide open.
> *(All half turn away in same direction and suggest movement
> of walking, bent forward as if carrying packs and rifles.)*

NARRATOR   And as we hurried through the weed-grown street
> *(All turn to look left and down at dog, following it with eyes
> as it crosses left to right in front of them over the next lines.)*

SOLDIER 1   A gaunt dog started up from some dark place and shambled
off

SOLDIER 2   On legs as thick as sticks

SOLDIER 1   Into the wood, to die

SOLDIER 2   At least in peace

SOLDIER 3   *(Step forward and speak direct to audience, apologetically)*
No one had told us victory was like this

SOLDIER 4   echo quietly)* Victory.

SOLDIER 1   Not one amongst us would have eaten bread before he'd
filled the mouth of the grey child

SOLDIER 2   That sprawl'd

SOLDIER 3   Stiff as stone

SOLDIER 4   Before the shattered door.
> *(All turn towards the direction of* SOLDIER 4 *on right as they
> say their line, so that all are finally looking down at the floor
> beside* SOLDIER 4.)*

NARRATOR   There was not one who did not think of home.
> *(All slump shoulders during the final line; two lower head
> and cover face or eyes, one slowly sinks to the floor, one
> turns slowly away; then freeze. All hold very still in final
> position for several seconds.)*

Using drama to interpret poetry, whether for exploration, improvisation
or performance, will involve the full spectrum of kinds of talk: in pairs,
groups and whole class, for purposes of exploring ideas, reaching consensus,
problem solving. More importantly, as a medium for interpreting poetry,
drama involves the whole person in what the critic D.W. Harding once called
'feeling comprehension', where physical, emotional and intellectual response
are simultaneously engaged.

8

Poetry and the visual

It may well be true that poetry first attracts us through our complex awareness of the roles of sound in its composition. At the same time, most poems encountered in school are likely to be written down. And it is true that most poems make strong appeal to our visual talents and responses.

One of the main approaches to work involving language in school is to use the senses, including sight. As a topic, 'Seeing' can take up a whole term, with its effects lasting over a full secondary curriculum and beyond. It can look at two aspects: what the visual has to state and what it has to suggest. It can tell the onlooker about shape, size, colour, movement, texture. It can also suggest relationships, attitudes, moods, and tone. A useful exercise is to provide some photographs or other pictures and ask pupils what they can see. They will often see what the picture is suggesting as much as what it is stating. You can develop this further by providing half a picture and discussing what could be in the other half. The results can be serious and fascinating – and when they are facetious, pupils know that they are playing imaginatively against the visual evidence in front of them.

The terms image and imagination are very close cousins. It is no accident that Wordsworth 'gazed and gazed' upon his beloved daffodils and then used them as an image of a joyous happening, recalled 'upon the inward eye'. Norman MacCaig talks of the things he sees and 'the short journey they make/to my skull's back' – where they are transformed by the feeling intellect into relationships of images. Much of our work is to do with that 'inward eye', that imaging sense.

This chapter explores four approaches:
1. How to encourage pupils to look at the settings of poetry.
2. How to explore the possibilities of presentation and display in poetry.
3. How to make visually significant poetry.
4. How to look at the visual in other poets' work.

In many instances, this work is ideal for sharing, but the visual can also be an occasion for privacy. It is good to see poetry re-established as a public medium which can be shared communally, especially through its sound and dance, but not all poetry has been written for oral celebration. Some has been produced for personal expression by the poet and for equally personal, reflective exploration by its individual reader and re-maker. There should be plenty of poetry available in which pupils can browse as individuals, if that is their wish at the time.

There is no logical sequence or single process which will guarantee pupils' recognising the importance of the visual in a poem. More pertinent is a child's personal 'psychologic', her or his own ways of responding. For some, the way in may be through their confidence and competence as artists. Some may prefer working through analogy, for instance through matching pictures to poems. Some may be best at talking about what they 'see' in a poem. These dispositions, whatever they are, are the best place to start.

The everyday setting

Mr. Weller's suspicion of poetry, which cropped up in the very first chapter of this book, was that, 'Poetry's unnat'ral'. His reason for his contempt was advertising:

> 'No man ever talked poetry, 'cept a beadle on boxin' day, or Warren's blackin', or Rowland's oil, or some o' them low fellows; never let yourself down to talk poetry, my boy.'

That is something akin to D.H. Lawrence's remark that poets had left their proper craft and gone to work for advertising agencies. Some teachers find that commissioning pupils to see just how much word play does go on in such aspects of 'the outside world' as advertising is a way into looking at its role in poetry. Work can be small scale – a ten-minute chat at the end of a lesson – or it can become a major topic with pupils seeing how widespread some of the visual features of poetry are in general culture.

1.   Shop names

The old convention of shops bearing the names of their owners is not entirely dead, but many play with their titles. Some rhyme – 'Top Shop' and 'Jean Genie'. Some play with alliteration – 'Jean Junction'. Some play with a punning homophone – 'Royal Male'. Some invent new words, such as the food shop rejoicing in the name 'Delicatique'. Some pun by using an image, as in the hairdressers named 'Heavenly Thatch'. Having younger pupils collect names and categorise what devices they are using and how they aim to affect us is one small-scale approach to exploring the role of visual word play.

2.   Advertisements

Many advertisements rely on their 'shape', the interplay of visual components of typography and layout with their language. Some advertisements exploit the pictographic, a form of punning communication which often appeals to younger pupils and can be seen as the first stage of shape and concrete poetry.

Carefully chosen advertisements in which pupils can find such features can be used for group discussion on how the effects were achieved, with groups going on to develop examples of their own. Later, this can be linked with the old trick of looking at a poem with the eyes half closed, so that the reader sees only its blurred shape and starts to think of what it might be signalling. 'Why do you think someone wrote this poem in four blocks, with the last two lines in each block longer than the rest and printed in a different typeface?' That can lead to discussion about the role of stanzas and how they can signal stages of development, rather like paragraphs, or can be subverted, if the poet wants to play with them. 'Why do you think this poem is written as one big, solid block?' could lead to an interesting discussion of the dreadful exhausted walk in Henry Treece's *Conquerors*. The technique has other potential gains. It can bring attention to the existence of the title, a feature so often ignored. It can also help pupils to explore much 'free verse'. 'Why is this poem so long and so thin with the last line written in capitals?' 'Why is this poem broken in two on the page?' This sense of visual shaping is usefully served by exploring advertisements.

3. Press headlines

Press headlines often use the visual to 'catch the eye'. For example, alliteration caught the eye as much as the ear with the cryptic headline:

TOOK TURKEY TO TOILET

Such terse headlines have another role to play in our work on poetry. They are full of informational gaps, and we have to take what has been called 'inferential walks' to complete them. Poetry often leaves similar space so that we can enter and partly furnish it ourselves. Young pupils enjoy working out what might have happened – in this instance, a poultry processor smuggling carcasses from the factory, a disappointing story! Quite often, the word play deliberately sets out to be expected as in the holiday accident:

TRIP THAT ENDED IN DISASTER

or the alliterative:

SICKNESS SCUPPERS SAILING ADVENTURE

or the obvious metaphor when two bowlers called Frost and Hudson were engaged in a local tournament:

HUDSON HOPING TO GIVE FROST THE SHIVERS

Building up a display over two or three weeks of such press cuttings can lead to discussion of the way many headlines try to be more than informational; how they suggest more than they state, often through a twin message; how they try to catch our eye by their layout and devices of word play – in other words how they try to use some of the features we also associate with poetry. More confident pupils can then see how poets often use these devices to create the unexpected rather than the expected – same device, different purpose – and can consider how far it is this trying to see things anew which makes poetry challenging.

4. Poems and verses

Poems, verses and rhymes still appear frequently in public forms, from the didactic or celebratory to the amusing or rude. Some magazines have the occasional reflective, 'improving' poem: Patience Strong must be among the best known writers of verse in Britain, especially since the women's magazines she has written in are not read solely by women. Some magazines have light verse in them as well. Such poetry tends to appeal to the ear with regular rhythms and rhymes, but it is usually also strongly imagistic, conveying through a series of word-pictures examples of the points it wants to make.

Special occasions are often celebrated through the 'special language' of poetry. *In Memoriam* and *Deaths* columns in newspapers often try to catch love and loss through a ritual couplet or verse. Happier occasions also encourage verse-writers – birthday and Christmas cards and special anniversary cards such as those for Valentine's Day and Mother's Day. It is interesting to note three basic styles – fairly formal prose; debunking humour; and verse – and to discuss who chooses which and why. Simple analysis of verses in cards can look at the images they contain and can lead to a discussion of how much we rely on expected images in these circumstances – mistletoe, holly, the fireside, the manger, the star at Christmas – whereas a lot of poetry relies on our being patient and getting excited about unexpected images. It can be worth comparing 'expected' images with the images that poets use more daringly to startle us into seeing things anew.

And then there is the use of verse for being rude – a time-honoured custom! The problems over using graffiti in the classroom – of vulgarity and a class 'going high' – are obvious. It may be safer to ignore this vigorous aspect of verse or to tackle it through accepted examples of the unrespectable, such as some of the profferings in Arnold Silcock's *Verse and Worse* (Faber) or books of satire and parody. In all of this, the aim is to show that many of the features at the disposal of the poet are at everyone's daily disposal as well.

Presentation

It is interesting to see how often reviews of poetry books for children pay particular attention to the layout and supportive illustration, recognising that the visual context of the poem can be significant. It can be interesting for older pupils to see how presentation has changed over the years, from the dignified print and layout of Victorian times to the interplay of print and illustration to be found in more recent times. School anthologies are one source for seeing how colour, picture and poem and matching typographical features have affected the poem. The Penguin *Voices* series and such anthologies as *Watchwords* and *Wordscapes* have all been popular for their use of layout and illustration. It is also worth exploring texts from beyond school: from illustrations in poetry books for little children to those by Willy Pogany for Edward Fitzgerald's classic version of the *Rubaiyat of Omar Khayyam,* or the illustrations that William Blake engraved and coloured for his *Songs of Innocence and Experience.* Other sources include the presentation of lyrics on sheet music and on the backs of records, and a comparison of poems as presented on the page and in poetry posters. In all instances, the remit is to consider the degree of 'fit' between the images in a poem and its visual presentation.

1. Picture box research

Looking at the way others have succeeded in creating a visual context for a poem can lead pupils to try the process for themselves. Groups can seek illustrations for a theme – Old Age, for instance, or Autumn or Towns or Joy. They can also be commissioned to create their own clusters of pictures on a theme of their own choice. These picture collections can then be used by their creators or by others as the basis for writing poems or for tracking down poems which link with them.

This can be turned round so that pupils are first of all presented with the poem or poems and are then asked to seek pictures which link in. Linking need not necessarily be supportive: some pupils may choose pictures which debunk or contradict. Illustrations can be ready-made or can be the pupils' own. Some pupils can become quite involved in such approaches to exploring the visual aspects of a poem, and it can be worth arranging for them to liaise with helpful colleagues in the Library and the Art Department.

Some schools have extensive resources with cross-referencing systems which make finding appropriate pictures a fairly speedy task. One school keeps pictures from newspapers, colour magazines and other sources in boxes with deliberately general headings. COLD, for instance, includes cold countries, creatures that live in the cold and the oceans. HOT includes hot lands, their flora and fauna, and anything to do with such fiery objects as the Sun, rockets and atomic energy. There is a PEOPLE box and a MISCEL-LANEOUS box. The system is intended to create discussion and even argument. Possible time-wasting can be overcome by setting definite tasks and time limits. For example, a group of four may be asked to sort out the poems and pictures for a theme to be tackled in a fortnight's time and be given access to the boxes for a single period of class time and half an hour over a lunch break. They are then expected to help mount the display and justify it when that theme is being discussed two weeks later.

2. Display

There are many ways of getting pupils to present their poem picture links to wider audiences. One is the graffiti sheet, a large sheet of display card or paper on which a class writes its best 'striking phrases' from its browsing in poetry books, the week's most striking visual headlines, worst puns, silliest riddles. The teacher's task is to keep the device under control, taking the sheet down between lessons if anyone has to change classrooms, and keeping the pupils focused on the visual. More easy to cope with is the poetry poster. Sometimes, professionally produced poetry posters are available from a Regional Arts Association or can be borrowed from local Teachers' Centre. Such posters can also be produced by the pupils themselves and offer an excellent chance for English and Art departments to liaise in helping pupils to express what they see in a poem in pictorial terms.

Younger pupils enjoy creating a frieze poem, either interpreting a long poem or weaving their pictorial commentary in with a poem that they have written. The results can be moving – a set of pictures to go with Coleridge's *Ancient Mariner* or a set of poems written to go with Victorian pictures of the poor. A class can also deliberately set out to create the worst possible stereotype image for a rhyming couplet frieze, to create a sponsored poem of utter awfulness!

Simple publications are an effective means of developing the sense of the visual in poetry. If a class works on haiku, for example, (see chapter 9) it should be possible to provide wall space for each child to display a haiku and an accompanying illustration. It is also worth having each child write a haiku on a Banda master or a sheet for photocopying. With care, you can get a class's work on two sides of A4 paper. The class might also wish to print a slightly less crowded publication and sell it to parents at a small profit, making enough over a term to provide the refreshments for an 'open' Poetry Browse towards the end of the summer term. Other ideas for A4 publication include snippets from pupils' poems over half a term, their 'striking phrases' collections on a particular theme, or their longer poems.

Poetry does not have to appear on flat paper. Art Department colleagues are full of good ideas for inventive linking and presentation. These can include devising models to accompany poems; setting poems against appropriate textures and colours of backgrounds; mounting such poems as haiku, so that they face an accompanying illustration making a sort of concertina – the eye seeing pictures from one direction and poems from the other. Poems can also be worked upon other materials – three images of the sea and its years of erosion of the land scratched on a flat pebble; images of autumn written with a fine felt-tip pen on leaves which are 'swirled' on a large window with dabs of latex glue – a transient picture poem. Some pupils have worked on a poem to accompany an object, seeking visual images to fit the object and the message – the dedication to be inscribed on a bracelet; a couplet to decorate the rim of a celebratory piece of pottery; a poem to act as the surround to a photograph or, as in Chinese art, to appear within the picture as a comment on it. The more opportunistic and encouraging such approaches are, the better.

The school magazine is probably the most common forum for display. Some schools also produce poetry magazines to show their best work. Both are useful ways of presenting poetry, but they are not enough. Encourage in-form and in-year publications in which everyone's work is recognised, for example through the inclusion of a poem, or a snippet on a 'best phrase' page, or a brief report on the main images of Valentine's cards verse, or a line sketch as a response to a poem.

Writing to see

So far, this chapter has looked at ways of raising awareness of the visual aspect of poetry and poetic uses of language. Alongside this opportunities can be created for pupils to write in order to focus upon the visual.

In making poetry which appeals to the visual, pupils can gain insight into the challenges of creating links between seeing and saying. There are many ways of doing this, and recommended books are listed in Appendix 3. But there are several simple initiatory tactics which are described here.

1.   Kennings

In Old Norse and Old English times, people enjoyed re-naming things so that they were seen anew, through riddles and kennings. Kennings were often used in poetry – a longship being called a 'foamy floater', the sea 'the whale's road', and so on. At their best, kennings caught shape, movement and tone. They also caught the poet's attitude towards what was being described – his awareness of the vastness of the sea or the horror of a dragon – 'loathly air-flier'. Children continue the tradition of riddle and pun and often enjoy a kenning competition. It can last for a mere ten minutes, re-naming one item or items in one category. Or it can last over a long time, especially if it is linked with work on striking images and phrases. One language project commissioned pupils to create kennings for things as varied as gravy, snake, fog, custard, toothpaste, shoes, happiness. One pupil re-named trees 'giant-weeds' and another twelve year old caught the melancholy of winter trees in 'sky beseechers'. Much lighter were 'footbags' for socks and 'handbags' for mittens. The visual component is often very explicit in early efforts at kennings, becoming more oblique and implied as pupils gain confidence in the power of words to suggest rather than state.

Seamus Heaney's version of the Middle English poem *The Names of the Hare* (RB) is really a cluster of seventy kennings, and pupils can follow suit by producing their own set for another creature or object. Pupils can invent amusing kennings for school subjects and more serious ones, perhaps, for moods or the 'seven ages'. One or two might wish to look at how often we use the visual in the form of kenning known as euphemism, using nice words to cope with or conceal the unpleasant – e.g. the 'mopping up' not of dirty water but of small groups of soldiers; the labelling of most civilians in a nuclear war exercise as 'brushwood' with those to be saved and protected known as 'tall trees'. Senior pupils might wish to consider the part the visual has to play in enabling language to suggest more than it states – so enabling us all to be 'poetic' in responding to the resonance of language.

2.   *X* is like

'*X* is like . . .' is an extension of kennings and our natural gift for identifying the new through using the already known – our gift for analogy, as used in simile and metaphor. This activity can be played as a limbering up exercise for a few minutes; it can also be used as a cumulative task, helping to provide focus by exploring connotations. Where denotation refers to the clear, unambiguous labelling of something, connotation relates to its associations, to what springs into one's mind, memory and emotions.

To carry out this activity, someone names something – an object, creature, mood – and everyone tries to create one or two visual comparisons or images. 'Being sad is like . . .' resulted in: 'having a boulder on top of you', and 'like your heart not being able to stand up'. With less confident pupils, you might want to introduce pictures which give a new vision of objects – in close-up, from an unusual angle, in unusual light. Pupils can then work out their comparisons from a shared focus. It is always worth showing pupils some similes and metaphors in action in poetry, especially those which help us to see anew, such as Elizabeth Bishop's description in *The Fish* (RB) of the ancient fish she caught, so old and battered that:

> Here and there
> his brown skin hung in strips
> like ancient wallpaper.

Senior pupils may find it interesting to look at earlier imagery, such as Ernest Dowson's use of metaphor in his Victorian melancholy.

> They are not long, the weeping and the laughter,
>   Love and desire and hate:
> I think they have no portion in us after
>   We pass the gate.
>
> They are not long, the days of wine and roses:
>   Out of a misty dream
> Our path emerges for a while, then closes
>   Within a dream.

Brighter pupils who become interested in imagery can link this with work on Victorian imagery in hymns, for example. In work on simile and metaphor, encourage pupils to produce their own. The results can be recorded on the blackboard or graffiti sheet or published on an A4 sheet.

Younger pupils sometimes have problems in progressing from simile to the density of metaphor. A useful tactic is to use Kenneth Koch's idea of reworking similes so that 'is like' and any direct denotative information about the subject are removed, turning the result into a riddle for others to solve. 'A fat sun', 'a glowing cricket ball', 'a disc slotting out of the ocean' were the results of this process, once 'an orange is like ...' had been deleted. You can extend this device by having pupils write in three columns. Column 1 contains the name of the object and the words 'is like'; Column 2 contains the simile. One pupil wrote, 'A crying baby is like/ a wailing pink cave.' Column 1 is then folded back so that it cannot be seen. Column 2's initial word is altered – adding a capital letter and perhaps changing 'a' to 'The', if the writer wishes. In this instance, the pupil wrote, 'The wailing pink cave' in Column 2, and, 'hiccupped and fell asleep.' in Column 3. Column 2, begun as a simile, is now a metaphor.

3. Shape poetry

One of poetry's rules is that it can disobey the rules of prose, if it wants to, and experiment with layout. Younger pupils enjoy looking at poems which are deliberately iconic, their shape acting as an image. George Herbert's devotional poem *Easter Wings* was written in the form of an angel's wings. Less seriously, Edwin Morgan's *French Persian Cats Having a Ball* plays with Shah, chat and chachacha dancing all over the page.

Many pupils will recall in junior school drawing an outline of a creature and then filling it with words. There is little point in repeating this in secondary school unless it is developed – for less able pupils, perhaps, siting a tiger's thoughts in its head, hunger in its belly, speed in its hind legs and temper in its tail. A more sophisticated task is to generate a mood or attitude. One teacher had a large sheet of display paper represent a block of flats. Each pupil created a character and wrote about him or her at a specific time of day – on waking; at the time of going to work, for those who had a job or task to go to; on a hot Sunday afternoon; on a chill winter's evening. The writing was deliberately brief, could be in first or third person and had to create pictures in the mind. It was written up on uniform pieces of paper which became the windows of the flats. Written over four or five weeks, these windows created a poetry dossier for each character, and led to further poetry, supportive artwork and drama involving the characters as they gossiped or dealt with events.

Older pupils can try more subtle versions which set out to image moods – loneliness, joy, sulkiness. One group created a series of people-shapes in a bus queue, the words presenting the thoughts of each character and making up the shape which betrayed or concealed what he or she was thinking. Some pupils prefer to get away from the obviously pictorial, creating abstract shapes to echo their poems and even creating three-dimensional poetry, although this can be time-consuming.

Finally, pupils can play with the visual clues of conventional poetry as it exploits an unexpected break in the middle of a line, a line running its meaning on into the next instead of stopping, even a sentence deliberately leaping from the end of one verse to the next for effect. A.S.J. Tessimond's *Cats* is a delightful example of playing with layout. Its sense-units are cat-like in their agile unpredictability, stopping and starting where they will, leaping the gap from one verse to another, ignorant of – or wilfully ignoring – the man-made rules and regulations of respectable verse.

> They slip, diminished, neat, through loopholes
> Less than themselves; will not be pinned
>
> To rules or routes for journeys; counter
> Attack with non-resistance; twist . . .

Let your pupils see the rest of that elegant poem for themselves in Tessimond's *Collected Poems* (see Appendix 1b).

4. Focused images

One of the most popular introductions to learning about imagery is writing haiku. The haiku is often seen as a model of terse Japanese elegance, and it is worth remembering that, because it can be introduced too early. It takes some sophistication to work towards such apparent simplicity, achieved only by paring away so much that its few images suggest rather than state. Discussion about stylised pictures in Japanese art and of the economy required in other poetry, such as kennings, may help to prepare some pupils to use so few words to affect the eye and the feeling intellect.

A haiku is a three-line poem, strictly speaking with five syllables in the first line, seven in the second and five in the third, each line containing an image which is affected by the others. Rhyme is irrelevant and feels obtrusive in so brief a poem. Traditionally, a haiku refers to a season and creates a mood through its visual imagery.

> The hot day shimmers.
> Swallows scythe the heavy air,
> Dark blades against the sun.

Older pupils should be encouraged to follow the rules; younger ones will have enough to do with getting a couple of evocative pictures into so short a space. Arthur Waley's translations from the Chinese can help pupils to feel the mood of some Eastern poetry and are usually available through your local library. Edward Thomas's brief *In Memoriam (Easter, 1915)* is an example of a British poet showing similar evocative simplicity.

> The flowers left thick at nightfall in the wood
> This Eastertide call into mind the men

Now far from home, who, with their sweethearts, should
Have gathered them and will do never again.

Poets of all cultures and times rely upon the visual. Shakespeare's famous description of the seven ages of man in *As You Like It* (Act 2, Scene 7) is a classic example of a set of focused images:

All the world's a stage,
And all the men and women merely players:
They have their exits and their entrances;
And one man in his time plays many parts,
His acts being seven ages. At first the infant . . .

. . . and so it continues. Older pupils can try updating the images and can create a seven ages of woman as well.

Other topics lend themselves to this approach and can be intensified in their visual focus if they are allied to synecdoche, the use of one feature to signify the whole. At a simple level, pupils can try writing a four-line celebration of the seasons, each line based on a tree and its seasonal foliage, on the sea and its temper in each season, on the passing seasons as they affect a city street. A more sophisticated task is to write a poem which does not have such an obvious imagistic structure. William Blake's *The Smile* is a good example to work from as it calls upon the reader to imagine each smile that it summons up – and each frown.

There is a Smile of Love.
And there is a Smile of Deceit,
And there is a Smile of Smiles
In which these two Smiles meet.

Senior pupils respond to the strong use of synecdoche in Dylan Thomas's *The hand that signed the paper felled a city* (RB).

The hand that signed the paper felled a city;
Five sovereign fingers taxed the breath,
Doubled the globe of dead and halved a country;
These five kings did a king to death.

The whole poem is an excellent starter for pupils as they experiment with similar focused imagery.

Some pupils enjoy writing from within the object or creature that they are describing. Sylvia Plath's *Mushrooms* (RB), for instance speak of how:

Overnight, very
Whitely, discreetly,
Very quietly
Our toes, our noses

Take hold on the loam,
Acquire the air.

This is a black humour poem which many pupils enjoy. They find working along similar lines liberating, since it provides them with a mask behind which to operate and through which to speak. It can therefore be a useful introduction to the idea of a poet working through a 'persona' as poets often do.

Discussing the visual in poetry

More formal academic approaches to the visual are discussed later. What follows here are some ways of promoting discussion which retain an element of game and grow naturally out of the other active approaches outlined in this chapter.

1. Filming

Many pupils are quite sophisticated in their knowledge of film techniques and will spend time working out how to script the filming of a poem when more conventional approaches would be labelled boring. It is worth having a simple assignment sheet duplicated on A4 paper for issuing to classes or groups when using this approach (see page 85). It saves organisation time. It can also be very handy for the occasional lesson, where you are asked to cover for a colleague.

Pupils use the boxes on the left to sketch out as simply as possible their visualisations of the poem. The right hand column includes the words from the poem which fit the sketch and which should accompany it as a voice-over. This column can also include comment on any sound effects or music or any other matter which helps to explain the interpretation of the poem. The middle column includes the instructions applicable to the camera crew:

WA	WIDE ANGLE	See a wide section of the scene.
FF	FULL FRAME	See a whole body or object.
HF	HALF FRAME	See smaller area, such as body from waist upwards.
CU	CLOSE UP	See area such as face or hands.
ECU	EXTREME CLOSE UP	See area such as mouth or eye.
P	PAN	Move camera in circular sweep, for example across horizon.
T	TRACK	Keep camera parallel to a moving object.
Z	ZOOM	Camera lens moves in towards ECU or CU (zooming in) or back towards FF (zooming out).

Picture	Film Instructions	Poem/Comment/ Music/Sound effects

Working in pairs, pupils can start with brief visual poems. Tennyson's *The Eagle* is useful.

> He clasps the crag with crooked hands;
> Close to the sun in lonely lands,
> Ringed with the azure world, he stands.

> The wrinkled sea beneath him crawls.
> He watches from his mountain walls,
> And like a thunderbolt he falls.

Older pupils find Henry Treece's *Conquerors* an interesting and accessible poem for this approach. As with many poems, they will find much of it easily filmable but there will be parts which cause problems. What to do with the title? What to do with the poem's final line? Such problems are ideal for discussion about what a poem can do that other media cannot. Senior pupils studying Philip Larkin, for example, will soon find out from this technique the points at which the poet 'changes gear' from describing events into metaphysical questioning and comment.

This is a technique which works with all ages, and it is interesting to see how often it leads to detailed exploration of a poem among pupils where conventional teacher-guided discussion would have gained little. Such work often has to remain at the 'pretend' stage, but if a video camera is available it can move on. Raymond Souster's amusing (and perhaps slightly disturbing) *Flight of the Roller Coaster* (Appendix 1a), for example, makes an excellent large-scale poster poem which can be video-recorded, complete with voice-over. Such work takes a great deal of time, but pupils see it as worthwhile activity from which they and the poem benefit.

2.   Stated and implied

This simple technique is best used initially with brief poems until pupils have become familiar with it. Choose strongly visual poems, such as George Mackay Brown's *The Hawk* (RB) which starts with the first day of the hawk's last week of life.

> On Sunday the hawk fell on Bigging
>   And a chicken screamed
> Lost in its own little snowstorm.

Pupils work on their own or in pairs, jotting down anything which the poem tells them through its visual detail on a printed sheet under two headings, *Stated* and *Implied*. Consider Tuesday in that poem when the hawk:

> fell on the hill
> And the happy lamb
> Never knew why the loud collie straddled him.

This technique can be used with poems about places or people. With less confident pupils it may be advisable to provide some kind of checklist to start their search. On places, they might see if there is anything said or implied about time of day or year, the weather, quality of light, natural and 'man-made' objects, and so on. A checklist to do with people might include their sex, age, actions, relationships, attitudes and moods. The results of such work can be used for discussion about what the poet has chosen to tell us and how. Asking pupils to seek information through small group discussion can give the teacher a chance to be diagnostic, to see pupils in action and to realise what they do – and do not – see in a poem.

Other techniques which exploit the visual are presented in the final chapter, on poetry as artifact. Any ways of attracting pupils into Wordsworth's 'gazing' should be welcomed. Sometimes a lesson finishes early, at least for some pupils. That can be a chance for them to track down a couple of poems which appeal to them visually for later work within the poetry agenda. Some pupils enjoy decorating or illustrating their poetry folders or introducing pictures from other sources. You may be lucky enough to work with an Art colleague who is also interested in poetry and who can contribute further ideas according to her or his expertise.

This chapter has discussed four main approaches: looking at the visual climate in which all language lives, including poetry; exploring the visual in the presentation and display of poetry; experiencing the task of harnessing the visual when writing poetry; seeing the visual in other people's poetry. But given that sight is so powerful a means of making sense of the inner and outer world, there are, of course, many more ideas than this chapter has suggested for pupils and teachers to devise and share.

9

Writing poetry

Throughout this book, writing has played a constant part in pupil activities – whether in jotting down their first impressions of a poem in order to discuss it; in making a running commentary on a poem as they produce a tentative film script; or in annotating a poem in order to devise the best means of celebrating it out loud. Writing has been used as an important means of thinking and feeling about poetry. But there is another use of writing which creates awareness of what poetry demands and provides – that is, writing one's own poetry.

This chapter sets out to suggest ways in which pupils from the early years of secondary school onwards can experiment with poetry as form. There will be many occasions when they will be moved intellectually and emotionally to write 'poetically' – where content and form come together. At its most genuine, this is proper 'creative writing', which may appear as prose, or in dramatic dialogue or in free verse. That is fine and is to be encouraged. At the same time, there is a place for pupils to experience and experiment with the energising dilemma that many poets have faced, of how to say the unsayable, to bring together content and form. T.S. Eliot once complained that words have a nasty habit of slipping and sliding and not staying still when a poet tries to write. Every now and again, however, their wayward energy is brought within a living form – energy and control meet, as in a dance, with each word 'at home / Taking its place to support the others . . .' It is how to promote this sense of ordered energy and economy through focused activities with younger classes that this chapter addresses.

In recent years there has been a steady increase in the range of practical activities designed to develop children's awareness of poetry, and in the different forms which can create this awareness of possible structures, from sentence chains to haiku. This has had the great advantage of making writing in certain poetic forms accessible to everyone. At best, it makes the process into a tangible craft rather than a divine inspiration. At worst, it can lead to meaningless filling-in-the-blanks exercises, word-games divorced from any insight into extended communication. The tension that poets have to struggle with between content and form should be a fascinating one for students to explore, and should lead to sympathetic awareness of this often irreconcilable struggle. To quote the American poet Robert Francis in his *Collected Poems*:

> Words of a poem should be glass
> But glass so simple-subtle its shape
> Is nothing but the shape of what it holds.

Senior pupils may wish to read some of the many poems about the process of writing poetry: Coleridge's *Frost at Midnight*, Jacques Prévert's *To Paint the Portrait of a Bird*, Ted Hughes' *The Thought-Fox*, Seamus Heaney's *Digging*. If they are actively engaged in writing their own poetry, they are more likely to be interested in seeing what others have to say about the creative process.

This chapter will focus on describing 'blueprints' for experimenting with poetic forms, but it must be emphasised that a poem's latent 'meaning' should not be sacrificed to an obsession with form. The aim is not to turn out writers of formulaic minor verse, but to 'cleanse the gates of perception' as William Blake once said. The workshop activities suggested in this chapter set out to help pupils to see their world more clearly by exploring it in words and to recreate their perception through an artistic form.

F.A.S.T.E.R. – an approach to pre-writing

The pre-writing stage is critical, since it is at this point that the major work will be done in guiding pupils towards focusing on an experience, exploring it in depth with sympathy, attempting to express it through direct or indirect description, and trying out effects which will communicate with an audience. The mnemonic FASTER – Focus-Appreciate-Sense-Tinker-Express-Revise – indicates possible phases in the compositional, pre-writing stage. While these are described at some length here, actual classroom practice will determine how much or how little time they might take.

FOCUS: concentrating on an object or experience through direct encounter or recollection, or through experience of other art forms such as reading literature, watching a film or listening to music.

In a class lesson it takes skill to encourage pupils to show their divergent responses. It can be done by asking pupils to jot down thoughts on their own as a first stage, without chatting to anyone else, emphasising spontaneity of thoughts, recollections, opinions and the free flow of ideas. If pupils talk at this stage then there may be a pull towards a convergence of ideas, leaving less room for individual perceptions. You might try asking pupils to close their eyes so that they can 'see' more vividly an experience on the 'cinema screen' in their heads – the process Wordsworth described when he wrote of the daffodils which he later saw 'flash upon that inward eye'.

APPRECIATE: considering the experience more closely and savouring it, trying to capture its essentials.

This stage will be helped by encouraging pupils to talk to others, make notes and draw pictures. Senior pupils can be encouraged to develop 'intertextuality' by comparing the experience with other literary passages and poems, or even exploring concepts with a thesaurus. Once pupils have taken a positive and personal stance, the next stage, of exploring their ideas with other people, should lead to greater clarity without their losing their individual perceptions as they encounter other viewpoints.

SENSE: recreating the experience or object using the senses, calling the experience into the mind's eye, making comparisons which widen and clarify its meaning.

This stage may begin with a whole class discussion on sensory experience – touch, taste, smell, sight, hearing. The senses make experience tangible as it is relived. Each of the senses has different dimensions to be explored. Sight, for instance, distinguishes the three dimensions as well as colour, texture, movement, size and shape. Touch focuses particularly upon texture, pressure and temperature, features which sight cannot always distinguish. Hearing, particularly in relation to the sound of the human voice can distinguish pitch, pace, tone, intonation and volume and, by implication, sex, age, dialect, mood, morale, temper, and so on. What the senses state and what they imply is a rich tapestry, to be explored first in a general discussion. The class may respond to prompts and signposts alone, without having to be instructed formally to run down a list and check it off item by item. Then pupils can move on to solo work again, recalling the sense impressions of their own particular experience and jotting down words and phrases as they occur. This recreation of the experience will add substance to the ensuing writing, when the experience is described through the abstract medium of language.

TINKER: inventive, adventurous playing with words and phrases, sound patterns, images, metaphors.

Words and phrases jotted down by individuals may be discussed in pairs, small groups or with the whole class. As part of the poetry curriculum there will be a place for word-games and for tinkering with possible formats: structures whose organising principle is line length or number of syllables, or which employ rhyme and rhythm schemes. First-hand knowledge of a wide range of technical effects is a great advantage to the young writer. This stage might be specifically targeted on a particular poetic technique or be open to whatever shaping the individual writers choose.

EXPRESS: drafting ideas in an extended form.

In this stage pupils again work on their own, on the first tentative draft of their poem. In spite of the usefulness of talk at certain stages of creative work, there is no doubt that silent concentration is at the heart of much creativity.

All may find it helpful to seek support from teacher or peer group, and resources such as poetry anthologies, thesaurus or dictionary. But there may be a conflict of interest between those who need absolute quiet and those who cannot resist the opportunity to talk. Some children may prefer to draft their poem at home, because they know they will find quiet there. It is advisable to develop a range of working conditions in class which includes silent private work. Those who are temporarily unable to write anything, for whatever reason, can always read, think, talk quietly with the teacher. Anything else is likely to distract the concentration of someone else.

REVISE: looking at the original 'vision' in the poem and redrafting it after further consideration – whether privately or with a partner, group or the whole class.

Pupils should experiment with words, their sounds, associations and effects, seeing them as akin to clay, to be moulded and shaped. Jottings in a rough book followed immediately by writing up a final version in an exercise book are not likely to encourage this sort of experimentation. Conditions and facilities which will create a positive climate for the courage and patience which redrafting demands include:

- advice to the class at an early stage that time will be allowed for several (e.g. three) drafts, to avoid the expectation of some pupils that quick results will be acceptable or expected.
- encouragement to use a rough book or separate sheets of paper for successive drafts, to avoid the fear of crossings-out in the 'best' book.
- scissors and a glue-stick to encourage 'cut and paste' editing on rough paper.
- a word-processor, with or without poetry-generator software, to make redrafting easier and more amenable to some.
- a typewriter so that a draft can be seen anew, in a 'published' form.
- a read-aloud partner for mutual constructive criticism.
- a delay between drafts, to allow for further thought.
- serious constructive commentary by a larger group or the whole class, who have been taught how to focus on 'what I liked best about this poem'.

There have been considerable advances in computer software. Some teachers will oppose the very notion of writing poetry on a computer using a 'poetry generator' program, on the grounds that this is not a creative process. But the extent of the creativity called for depends entirely on how the program is written. Some programs will be little more than filling-in-blanks worksheets rewarded by flashing lights; but others, within flexible guidelines, may have all the openness of word-processing. Here the screen is greatly more adaptable than a sheet of paper, in that infinite word-play and revision is possible without the need for clumsy deletion; and the final poem is printed out, which looks very professional. Some children become highly motivated when using this medium for writing. That alone makes it a worthwhile resource, in spite of any traditional reservations an adult might have. Another feature is that the processor, with its large screen, allows collaborative writing, with several pupils suggesting ideas, and the words and phrases which might best express them.

Towards a sense of form through writing

Ideally writing poetry will be a regular component of the poetry agenda in the classroom; not just an occasional one-off to end the term or as a change from the usual homework. Only with frequent practice will children become fluent as creators. Where that is the case pupils will be aware of a range of possible forms into which to weave their perceptions. But where it is not common, and where there is no careful guidance as to the form and shaping processes of poetry, poetry writing will remain the province of the few.

Confidence will also come from frequent encounters with a wide range of poetry. The best motivation to write is likely to come in response to other poems. Poems understood and enjoyed act as 'models' for pupils' own writing, not in slavish imitation but as springboards. Younger pupils often 'echo' features of other people's writing. This is not plagiarism but an intuitive recogniton on their part of insights and expressions which have moved them. If these appear in their own efforts to explore poetic form, so much the better. The weekly poetry comprehension exercise is not to be recommended. It is likely to set up negative associations of poetry as an arcane mystery and as a test. If pupils build up a repertoire of poems *they* have explored and enjoyed, often on their own terms, they will have many more models for their writing, and more ways into viewing and expressing their own experiences.

1. Free verse

'Free verse' was perhaps the first form in recent times to be widely adopted for the 'new' poetry teaching, as for instance in the Creative Writing movement. Much has been gained where this approach has not been used crudely to mean a 'stimulus' for 'vivid' writing, and has genuinely invited pupils to write reflectively and honestly. But the mistaken perception that 'free verse' is absolutely free can be the most oppressive of tyrannies for many students. So many cultures recognise the pulse of language in their attempts to give expression a form that an insistence on avoiding it can be counter-productive. For instance, the strong rhyme and rhythmical patterns of nursery verse and the strong rhythms (and, occasionally, rhymes) of lyrics are deeply imprinted in many pupils, so that when you speak of writing poetry it is those patterns which come to the surface. Our minds can never be truly free of others' thought patterns, and the blank sheet of 'free verse' with its demand that the poet create form by some other device, such as a recurrent image, is not a strong enough pattern on its own to override more familiar patterns.

The options available in free verse need to be 'taught' as much as caught. The most positive way to teach any pattern is by the example of published poetry – the more the better. Pupils should be commissioned to find examples of free verse which they enjoy and to try to sort out what makes them attractive. Because it is 'free', free verse can experiment with an infinity of patterns, but certain features of free verse should be observable, worth discussing and worth experimenting with. One of the most obvious is the appeal to a reader's visual sense by playing games with layout: a conventional layout or an unconventional one; a long, thin poem winding across a page; words written with no gaps between them; a single word on a line of its own for dramatic effect; a change of type face. There are simple, clear and easily demonstrated effects which pupils can then readily imitate. A free verse poem may well also give itself some shape, or subvert it, through its exploitation of sound: its deliberate insistence on prose, perhaps in dialogue; its play with onomatopoeia, assonance and alliteration; its use of repetition and even of nonsense sounds. Playing with words and phrases in the 'Tinkering' stage will encourage pupils to find such patterns as they work their perceptions into language. Similarly, visual and sensory patterns created through imagery, simile and metaphor, may be recognised by calling images on to the cinema screen of the mind – perhaps through an injunction to 'close your eyes and relive it'.

By implication, then, 'free verse' may be appropriate for some younger pupils as a form in which to write with a certain naïveté. It is also obviously an area for much deeper exploration with senior pupils. Free verse forms tend, perhaps, to be not particularly conventional among many of the poets who senior pupils are expected to study. That is a pity, since free verse, at its best, requires the poet constantly to invent new rules for new games and demands a particularly alert and responsive reader in return.

Younger pupils in the secondary school may well have met various poetic conventions already, but it is worth revisiting them, so that pupils become more adept in their use. The following suggestions outline some approaches which have proved particularly accessible.

2.   One focus per line

The notion that a poem aims at achieving some overall shape is perhaps the most difficult to guide younger pupils towards. Some are likely to worry and ask of their efforts, 'Is this poetry?' Such advanced internal structural features as a recurrent motif implied and echoed through chains of images, or links created through sound effects, or the use of dramatic heightening may well be present in even a young pupil's writing. But some children yearn for a more obvious 'poetry' shape than that, and they might find 'one focus per line' a useful initial guideline from which to develop and, eventually, deviate.

The struggle between content and form can be played with as a game if you offer an outline shape which provides a focus for each line. For instance, the guidelines for a free-verse four-line poem on 'Autumn' might run:

Line 1 – Give a general description of a panorama.
Line 2 – Zoom in on a specific detail within that scene.
Line 3 – See yourself or some other person in the scene.
Line 4 – Set a mood associated with the scene, either stated or implied.

This produced, for example:

> A chill east wind sweeps over bare fields,
> Bending the tattered rushes by the ditch's edge.
> Collar up, head down a labourer hoes between green shoots
> Sweeping in hope a path for spring to walk.
>
> (S. J. Parker)

Such a highly prescriptive approach can be enabling for some pupils, though others may find it a straitjacket and even an impossibility. Where that is the case, especially when they have other ideas, let them go! Discussing what the technique enabled pupils to do – or prevented them for doing – can lead to greater awareness of the content-form tension and the energies it can create.

3.   The five W's

A less prescriptive outline for the 'one focus per line' approach is offered by the five 'W' questions in this pattern:

line 1   who
line 2   what
line 3   where
line 4   when
line 5   why

For instance in this example:

> Frost
> Etches strange patterns
> On window panes
> In silent moonlight
> To tell us of another world.   (S. J. Parker)

A simpler structure is offered by Shakespeare's 'Crabbed age and youth', through the alternating contrasts between two opposites:

> Crabbed age and youth
> Cannot live together:
> Youth is full of pleasance,
> Age is full of care;
> Youth like summer morn,
> Age like winter weather;

Youth like summer brave,
Age like winter bare.
Youth is full of sport,
Age's breath is short ...

4. List poems

The song lyrics, 'These are a few of my favourite things', are perhaps the best known example of this type of one-focus-per-line poem. The title gives the central concept or organising principle, and the lyrics list line by line the images, associations and sense impressions which make the concept concrete. The pattern is very easy to parody, but Rupert Brooke's '*These I Have Loved*' is a classic example of a serious poet using the form. John Clare's richly sensuous *Pleasant Sounds*, being more in the form of notes than in polished rhyming form, is perhaps easier to imitate:

> The rustle of leaves under feet in woods and under hedges;
> The crumping of cat-ice and snow down woods and rides,
> narrow lanes and every street causeway;
> Rustling through a wood or rather rushing, while the wind
> halloos in the oak-top like thunder;

A rather more elaborate version of the list poem is where not just the introductory structure but other linking phrases are given as a framework into which ideas are fitted, to make more sophisticated contrasts. This was first developed in the book *Beat not the poor desk* by Marie Ponsot and Rosemary Deen (Boynton/Cook 1982). An example of this technique might be:

> The important thing about ...
> Is that it is ...
> It is true that it is ... and ... and ...
> But the important thing about ...
> Is that it is ...

However so much is done for the writer in this kind of formula that it could be uncreative for some pupils.

The nursery rhyme pattern of the old woman who swallowed the fly is well known, with its repetitions and list of what was swallowed. The anonymous 'This is the key' is a similar but less fantastic pattern, with a riddle embedded in it:

> This is the key of the kingdom:
> In that kingdom there is a city.
> In that city there is a town.
> In that town there is a street.
> In that street there is a lane.

And so it goes on until it turns back on itself and ends:

> Lane in the street.
> Street in the town.
> Town in the city.
> City in the kingdom.
> Of the city this is the key.

Ted Hughes' *Amulet* is a list poem with a similar progression, but the use of images loaded with symbolic meaning makes it a very sophisticated use of the medium:

> Inside the wolf's fang, the mountain of heather.
> Inside the mountain of heather, the wolf's fur.
> Inside the wolf's fur, the ragged forest ...

5.   Pastiche

'Pastiche' has echoes of a pasting together, of a patch job, but it can also be a serious and useful activity. It picks up current learning theory about 'modelling'. A teacher can tell a class how to do something, but instruction on its own does not usually result in successful swimmers, for example. A class can be given a quick demonstration, without commentary, but this is unlikely to be much more effective. Or there can be a demonstration with an accompanying interactive commentary, a dialogue among all those present. This is the ideal form of 'modelling'. In this instance, a poet has written a text which talks to a reader; the reader talks back – i.e., generates a version of that poem – and may well talk with other people, teacher and peers, about what is going on as the poem comes into being. In these circumstances, pastiche is certainly worth exploring, especially with senior pupils.

A pastiche is usually a poem written in serious imitation of a published form – parody is a form of pastiche which makes fun of the original. Clearly the process of imitation gives the writer the advantage of confidence in the structure and the challenge of responding fairly faithfully to it and the mood of the original. Younger pupils may not always catch the form, but it is interesting how often they will catch a poem's tone, as in this pastiche by a twelve-year-old of the John Clare passage quoted above. It is called *Autumn Evening*:

> The rooks as grave as lawyers sound
>   as I gather brittle wood
>   and hear the twigs' sharp snap
> The crisping crunch of trampled leaves
>   and the woodpecker's tap tap tap.
> The crisp evening haunted air
>   forms mist in the faded light

> While the screech and flap of startled birds
> Encourages the vixen's flight.

Pastiche is a powerful means of generating a sense of a poem as artefact. Further techniques for senior pupils are described in Chapter 10.

6. Concrete poetry

Long before coming to secondary school, many pupils will have had fun with early forms of concrete poetry such as the calligram (sometimes called 'Wordles') where a single word is made to express its meaning visually, e.g. long little, or they may have created the outline of an object and filled it in with descriptive words and phrases. Concrete poetry starts to become more sophisticated when the descriptive words alone complete the shape of the object described. Try this with such classic subjects as: a clock's spring, a tree, fireworks, a snake, a ghost train. Concrete poetry is a form of visual pun which is less popular than it was two decades ago. If you decide to use it, show children published examples after they have produced their own, so that they can create freely first and then from a position of positive achievement be able to appreciate the strengths and weaknesses of someone else's creation.

7. Syllabic forms

There are occasions when experimenting with an adaptation of an alien poetic form can help to highlight the importance of 'shaping' in poetry across cultures and across time. With its sense of economy, its ability to suggest more than can be stated, within a rigid formulaic discipline, Japanese poetry is a useful tool for younger and senior pupils.

Haiku

Of the syllabic forms it is haiku which has become the best known in recent years, perhaps its strongest appeal being its brevity; simply three lines totalling 17 syllables in the pattern 5, 7, 5 syllables. Some pupils find this a welcome relief from lengthy transactional prose. Its simplicity is, of course, deceptive, but the natural objects and sharp contrasts which are character-istic have wide appeal. Pre-writing should concentrate on clear visualisation – focusing on an aspect of nature, seeing two contrasting images which then imply an emotional state. It is also possible to write haiku as a series, as did Anthony Thwaite in his 12 poem sequence *A Haiku Yearbook* which has a haiku for each month of the year. Younger pupils can achieve much in this compressed form:

> Early in the day
> Admiring the morning
> The sun is shining.

Frail like an old man
The tree in the meadow stood
Waiting for nightfall.

In front of me I
See a picture created
By a haiku poem.

Tanka

Tanka is usually described as an extended form of haiku, made up of 5,7,5,7,7 syllables. However its origin has a much more satisfying story to it than that. Originally, amongst Japanese courtly circles, it was the custom to give a haiku to a noble friend as a way of sharing an insight into the natural world. The friend would add two additional 7 syllable lines to the haiku as a response and to create a new shared poem – a tanka – to celebrate the friendship between the two. The tanka is an emblem of the shared creativity which is promoted throughout this book. Clearly then our classrooms should take up this time-honoured custom and make every haiku into a tanka, according to the true spirit of poetry!

Sijo

A longer form based on the same principle is the Korean 'sijo', which is made up of six lines, each of either 7 or 8 syllables, hence totalling between 42 and 48 syllables. Again the subject is the natural world, emphasising the visual, emotional response, and using contrasting images.

8.   Line-length patterns

Cinquain

Some verse forms create their pattern by specifying a number of words for each line. The cinquain is made up of five lines but with two possible approaches to the line length: one takes the number of syllables, the other the number of words per line. Pupils can choose whichever they prefer:

line 1   1 word or 2 syllables
line 2   2 words or 4 syllables
line 3   3 words or 6 syllables
line 4   4 words or 8 syllables
line 5   1 word or 2 syllables

The brevity of the last line gives it a dramatic effect, as in this example (with apologies to William Carlos Williams)

Mum
I ate
The last peach
Left in the fridge.
Thanks!

There is an alternative pattern:

Noun

adjective   adjective

verb   verb   verb

4-word-phrase

noun

Here is an example:

Peach

fragrant   luscious

smell   taste   savour

memories of golden days

summer

Diamante

So called because of its shape on the page, the diamante is a simple pattern formed by fitting words into slots according to parts of speech. Although simple, it is nevertheless capable of subtle intricacies of meaning. The shape particularly suits a contrast between two related but opposing concepts: sun and moon, day and night, cat and dog. The increasing then decreasing line length encourages an expansion and development of one idea, before at the midway point there is a crossover, which leads to a quickening of pace as the lines shorten again towards the emphatic statement of the last line. The pattern runs as follows:

Noun 1

adjective   adjective

-ing   -ing   -ing

synonym 1 synonym 1 : synonym 2 synonym 2

-ing   -ing   -ing

adjective   adjective

noun 2

Perhaps this is best illustrated with an example:

Cat

clever   cuddly

crouching   pouncing   purring

meows   feline   :   canine   bark

running   sniffing   yelping

lovable   smart

Dog

Skilled writers can make up endless variations on this basic pattern playing with mood from the sentimental to the sardonic:

Sun
gorgeous   golden
glinting   gleaming   glowing
beach   easy-chair   :   after-June afternoon
browning   bronzing   broiling
pal o'mine   calomine
Sunburn   (S. J. Parker)

Teachers should be seen to write alongside pupils, facing the same challenges and taking the same risks. This is essential if the climate for poetry is to be one in which everyone is supportive because everyone is vulnerable – including the teacher.

All such formulae are best treated as guidelines only, offering licence to embellish or develop the pattern as pupils choose. Whether the results are what a purist would call 'poetry' is problematic; but such formulae allow children to play with words and enjoy the shaping process from which confidence with more flexible and intricate poetic forms might develop. Such simple guidelines usually help most children to 'succeed' – a very desirable target in poetry writing, which by its imprecise nature can be elusive for younger pupils in the secondary age range.

9. Traditional forms

Much learning is caught rather than taught: we learn by example and attempts at imitation. This can begin with attempts to inhabit fairly basic, traditional forms of poetry, starting with those which have a clear structure and a strong sense of rhyme and rhythm as a result of their origins in the popular oral tradition.

Ballad

The ballad is usually made up of a series of four-line verses, often with one or both pairs of alternate lines rhyming (*abab*). In its traditional form it usually tells a tale; so it is important in the pre-writing stage that the story should be worked out from beginning to end. A refrain, acting as a commentary on the events, is an attractive feature which can be added. One of the benefits of the ballad form is that groups can take on the task of writing one or two verses of the overall tale. At the end, the verses can be strung together and, with the collaboration of the music department, given proper life with a musical accompaniment. Pupils may also find it appealing to use song lyrics as models, looking first at those which tell a story in the ballad tradition. Songs by Bob Dylan and the Beatles have been much used for this; Ralph MacTell's *Streets of London* is a more recent example. The *Penguin Book of Ballads* has many examples of all types, from the humorous to broadsheet murder ballads which were very popular in early centuries.

Here is the first verse of a broadsheet ballad by a thirteen year old:

Black Jack is his name.
Murder is his game.
All the church bells rang
When Black Jack had to hang.

The final version was written out on paper which had been stained to look like parchment, with the edges charred and at the bottom there was a seal and ribbon – not entirely authentic in terms of a printed ballad but a very attractive piece when displayed. The rhyming couplets used here are probably easier to handle than the *abab* scheme since each line is linked more directly to the next. That simpler pattern is acceptable, and there seems little point in being purist about the form if children are choosing creative alternatives which are accessible but still prove sufficiently challenging.

Limerick

Playing with verse forms need not always be so serious or melodramatic a business. The limerick is quite a demanding pattern in that it has a set rhythm, together with a rhyme scheme. The original Edward Lear model is much easier since the last line repeats the first, which is conventionally pre-set as 'There was a young/old person of...' This gives the writer a formulaic start – although not everyone will find that helpful. It is also a forgiving pattern in that irregularities can add to the humour. Limericks are at their best when read aloud for their humour and their whimsical ideas.

Sonnet

Senior pupils can also find the task of exploring a specified form challenging. The sonnet has a long history and so there are many examples to read, with alternative structures for the rhyme scheme within the overall fourteen-line length. Perhaps the easiest is the Shakespearean sonnet, which is made up essentially of three phases of four lines each (rhyming *abab*) with a final couplet, the overall pattern being: *abab cdcd efef gg*.

Pupils should be able to explore sonnets in this form, to see how an idea can be developed across the initial three phases or how three images can be created to focus on a central theme, with the couplet summing up the key point or adding a twist to the poet's and the reader's understanding of the rest of the poem.

The Petrarchan structure is slightly more difficult, with two verses of four lines and two of three lines, the overall pattern being: *abba abba cde cde*.

Pupils should be encouraged to experiment with writing within either form, to see the demands that it makes on the process of shaping – the shape of each phase and its contribution to the complete pattern; the metrical shape as each line tries to fit the convention of iambic pentameter (with, perhaps, the closing lines being one foot longer); the sound shape as the line ends fit the rhyme scheme. That is a lot to juggle with and may need support, from peers or from the teacher. It is interesting how many senior pupils will try out such a structure as a sonnet and produce verse which is more than that, which moves into being poetry.

10.   Modern forms

'Free' verse, which has already been discussed, is used by many contemporary poets as are more 'traditional' verse forms. But at the same time, there are some poets who seek to find further forms in which poetry can thrive.

Word-play

Because poets are intrinsically inventive, the body of poetry available to us is continually expanding and developing, and so the number of forms which pupils can imitate or employ in their own writing becomes increasingly extensive. If teacher and classes have access to interesting books of poetry and have time to browse, they will never be short of new models for writing. Consider, for instance, this beautiful evocation of New England countryside by the American poet Robert Francis, in *Silent Poem*. By simply listing compound nouns with an evocative quality he builds up a total picture like an impressionist painter using dots of paint:

Backroad	leafmold	stonewall	chipmunk
underbrush	grapevine	woodchuck	shadblow
woodsmoke	cowbarn	honeysuckle	woodpile
sawhorse	bucksaw	outhouse	wellsweep
backdoor	flagstone	bulkhead	buttermilk
candlestick	ragrug	firedog	brownbread
hilltop	outcrop	cowbell	buttercup
whetstone	thunderstorm	pitchfork	steeplebush
gristmill	millstone	cornmeal	waterwheel
watercress	buckwheat	firefly	jewelweed
gravestone	groundpine	windbreak	bedrock
weathercock	snowfall	starlight	cockcrow

Francis said of his writing, 'I was and am fascinated with words themselves, their shapes and sounds', which provides the key to approaching this kind of structure. An ideal pre-writing activity for such poems would be to encourage word-play, drawing up lists on the board or in rough books, with groups brainstorming around a theme — try 'playground games', for instance. This particular form can be adapted to create interesting concrete poetry. You might also use dictionaries or better still a thesaurus to check out possible word choices. Other examples along the same lines are Hilaire Belloc's *The Frog* which draws together different names for the frog and Seamus Heaney's *The Names of the Hare* (RB).

Sense impressions

Poems which provide a kaleidoscope of sense impressions offer a lot of scope for imitation and can act as an evocative stimulus. Take for instance Carl Sandburg's *In a Breath* (Appendix 1a), which creates a sense impression of hot summer in Chicago, cleverly contrasting it with images of coolness in a movie showing at the cinema. In form it is almost prose; so it is not technically demanding, and the writer can concentrate on the sense impressions.

A.S.J. Tessimond's *A Hot Day* is a summer scene more familiar to British readers. Again it is the compilation of sense impressions which gives the poem its vividness, but Tessimond plays also with the sounds of the words, picking up alliterations and half-rhymes to weave a melodic sound-picture as well. For example:

> Sunlight weaves in the leaves,
> Honey-light laced with leaf-light.

Raymond Wilson's *Midnight Wood* uses the repeated structural pattern of a question to begin each stanza, slightly modified each time it is used, to build up a ghostly atmosphere:

> Dark in the wood the shadows stir:
>   What do you see?

The answer given is an evocative list of items, partly realistic, partly fantastic:

> Mist and moonlight, star and cloud.
> Hunchback shapes that creep and crowd
>   From tree to tree.

One way to handle this poem in class, so as to lead into personal writing, is to read the first verse complete to the class, to set the atmosphere. Then read just the first two lines of the next stanza to the class – a question in each case – and ask them to write down what they think of. Continue this for each verse, and either read them the 'answer' – what the poet wrote – or give them time to work up a clearer word-picture before reading the whole poem to them. That way they can compare their own vision with that of the poet.

Alliteration revisited

Alliteration rather than rhyme was a frequently used pattern in early poetry. Both *Beowulf* and *Sir Gawain and the Green Knight* are well known examples. In more recent times Wilfred Owen's *From My Diary July 1914* uses alliteration in tandem with a half-rhyme pattern:

> Leaves
>   Murmuring by myriads in the shimmering trees
> Lives
>   Wakening with wonder in the Pyrenees

Birds
  Cheerily chirping in the early day
Bees
  Shaking the heavy dews from bloom and frond ...

What makes this a manageable pattern for young writers is above all the use of a key word which is then developed in the next line. A practicable teaching approach is to:

- focus on the material to be explored
- list key words associated with it
- place them in an order or sequence of some kind
- add a single line description to each key word, concentrating on sense impressions
- tighten up the pattern of alliteration and/or half-rhyme throughout the poem.

Responding to pupils' poetry

Although some pupils will sometimes produce a poem of uniformly high quality, it is more usual for there to be flashes of insight and striking effects mingled with cliché or clumsiness. We all respond best to positive encouragment. So any response should be to the overall work and what it has shared with its readers. There should be no immediate dismantling. The moments in every poem which stand out exist within an overall text and should be acknowledged within that context. If the focus is on aspects of language and response, and is followed by encouragement, this should have a motivating effect. This focus should not be solely by the teacher or always on individual pupils' work. Pairs, small groups, the whole class, other classes, parents, the school magazine editorial panel and readership – all can have a part to play in responding to the poetry writing of individual pupils. The more sympathetic the reception the better: in some instances the role of the teacher will be to guide the criticisms of others towards positive rather than negative statements. Groups of children need training in this: one way is to tell them, when meeting to discuss each other's poetry, to list at least three things that they think worked well in the poem, before they go on to list two things at most that they might have done differently.

1. Marking

Poetry was not written to be marked or graded and there is no more justification for marking poetic efforts by pupils than there is in giving Wordsworth an A minus for achievement and an A plus for effort in writing *The Prelude*. In some schools, alas, there may be no choice: pupils are to be given a grade for every piece of written work. Where the teacher has a choice, it is far better for the poem to be responded to as appreciatively as possible, not just by the teacher but by other readers, orally as well as in written comments. This reflective, supportive, interactive approach to marking is in line with the approach to poetry teaching advocated throughout this book. Its worth is in what the writer learns from the writing and from the response of the readership.

2.   Challenges

There are occasions when writing will be free-ranging and even private, but there are others when it can be a challenge to extend the boundaries beyond personal expectations – and limitations. It is helpful to establish with pupils before they begin to write what their targets are for their written work – both what the writer is to focus on and, therefore, what the reader will be invited to discover. You can agree the focus with them in discussion, so that it plays an explicit part in setting the targets for the writing. At the same time those targets will be present implicitly in the patterns of the published poems read in class.

The challenges set will vary from one piece to the next. In specifying them, first of all there is the division between content and form; what the writer is saying and how it is said. You might want to establish a specific focus for the content: its meaning, tone, and the writer's attitude to the subject. As for the form, here the guidelines are more likely to be successful where they are narrowly focused, emphasising a particular aspect rather than a battery of skills. For instance, there might be a focus on imagery or rhyme, alliteration or onomatopoeia.

3.   Active response

Clear understanding of these guidelines will sharpen the readers' commentary on the work. But there are interim stages which might help the writing process. The first stage of a few minutes of solo-planning – jotting down of phrases, flash-images, sense impressions in notes – might usefully be followed by paired discussion, then followed by a discussion with the whole class. Such a sequence allows children to experiment and try out ideas in comparative safety, before they commit themselves to a larger audience, and it allows the teacher to check whether they have got the right idea about where the poem is to go.

Although children do not usually like writing successive drafts of their work, poetry is usually relatively brief, and the notion of craftsmanship more apparent. At any stage during the drafting individual writers can be given help by:
- the teacher going around the class advising
- reference to a dictionary or thesaurus
- conferencing with a partner
- reading out snippets to the class or a group for comment.

Once a draft has been completed there can still be a stage for suggestions which writers can accept or reject.

Presentation

When a poem is completed, a presentation of some kind, a display or a reading, may round off this interactive process. Pupils' own poems may be read out as a performance to the whole class, by the writer or a friend or the teacher. Clearly this is better if rehearsed. Other audiences might be:

- younger children in the school or the local primary
- a school assembly
- a lunch-time performance in school
- a parents' evening
- a local old people's home
- a local poetry festival.

It is important to encourage pupils to take a pride in how they present the words that they have crafted. High standards of presentation are tangible, and likely to have a carry-over into more abstract aspects of their work. The best poetry writing is likely to come from a classroom climate where children are encouraged to be adventurous towards their craft, taking risks and taking care equally at all stages; where their writing is treated with respect by themselves and others; and where good work is enjoyed by everyone through performance or display. Where they are working on single sheets of file-paper carried over from lesson to lesson, work will become dog-eared and scruffy unless it is kept in a proper folder – this can be a work of art in itself, as younger pupils often enjoy decorating a folder.

Writing out a final draft in best script is only one possible final stage, but clearly it is as important as a presentation 'live' or on tape, for example. Some pupils are always interested in experimenting with the shape of different scripts, different artistic layouts, illustrated lettering, and so on. Where there is no tradition of this kind, you might encourage typing out poems to make a class book. Seeing poems in print lifts the significance of their work, making them look at it in a new light and giving them a sense of achievement. The word processor has an important part to play in presenting 'perfect' copy of poems, just as it can be used as a valuable editing tool during a poem's gestation. It can also have a powerful role to play, particularly where a group of pupils chooses to write a poem together, such as a ballad or a protest song, pooling their emotions and thoughts.

10

Towards Artifact

Artifact. A thing made by art.

(Oxford English Dictionary)

The constant theme of this book has been that poetry was not written to be taught. It was written – is being written – to move the head and the heart through the experience and reflection of the reader. The earlier chapters have suggested that there is a constant interplay between what reader and poem have to say to one another about 'life' and what reader and poem have to say to one another about the poem itself as an experience.

That is where the sense of the poem as artifact comes in. It is good that pupils no longer have to apply labels mechanistically to poetry but can choose from a range of active approaches which encourage more personal, considered response. Nevertheless, many pupils do find delight in exploring how a poem has been shaped and senior examinations still seek some evidence of pupils' awareness of 'form' as a feature of poetry. Some young people will not continue to advanced and university studies in literature; but there are those who will. In either case, the 'gaming' approaches which this chapter describes cater for students who are becoming aware of the poem as artifact. It is interesting to see the increasing use of such techniques with students in university English faculties, as lecturers become more familiar with them and recognise their potential in developing intellectual rigour as well as openness of response.

In Appendix 3 there are the titles of some books which are particularly valuable in helping pupils to understand artifact by creating their own poems – by experiencing being poets themselves. This chapter focuses on enabling pupils to see in action the skills of *poiesis*, shaping, in other peoples' poems. It describes a sample of approaches which grow from work described earlier on in this book. Several of the techniques it outlines can be used with younger and less able pupils, but the main principle in selecting them has been to show approaches which will stretch the gifted and mature as well. All pupils are capable of some degree of abstraction and awareness of structure and form;

all are aware of language as symbolisation. The rest of this chapter shows how this awareness can be developed by collaborative devices. It is worth remembering that some senior students may well wish to adapt these approaches for private study and reflection as well.

The study of skilled crafting in other people's poetry has always been part of our work in the literary curriculum. In a sense, it is only bringing into focus at a more advanced level the very young child's naive awareness that even such early poems as nursery rhymes are somehow different from other uses of language; that someone is playing special games with language for a special purpose. It is good to encourage our pupils to enjoy recognising skill and craft in action wherever they can, including in a poem. The problem comes when we insist that they explore such craft on only one set of terms, those inherited from classical prosody. 'Dactyl' and 'spondee' and other Ancient Greek terms for structural features can be objects of great fascination for some pupils and help them to explore a poem's artifice with increasing appreciation and delight. But an insistence that, towards the top end of secondary education, pupils must explore the way poems have been made mainly through such labels, without looking at motives and effects, can cause confusion. Worse, it can make poetry mysterious and inaccessible, something it was never intended to be. Appendix 2 contains a brief selection of terms which senior pupils might want to explore and which you might want to refer to, as certain points of technique arise in an exploration of a poem. The glossary is written for students to read and sets out to show possible links between technique and effect in poetry. There is no more justification for denying pupils access to these concepts than there is for imposing them. Introduce them when the time is right to those pupils who would enjoy experimenting with them. Use them as a basis for further exploration with those who are prepared to go further. That does not mean introducing such terms as 'synecdoche' only to very bright pupils. Whatever our level of intelligence, we make practical use of synecdoche and spondee, and as for the 'feeling intelligence' which we use to respond to a poem, that is a talent which everyone possesses.

Poem as pattern – virtual simultaneity

It is useful to think in other ways about how a poem is made. For a start, most poems are short – far shorter than stories. That means that they are often far more compressed than a prose story. The words have to get on with one another far more than words in the greater living space of a long novel. In poems, most words work hard for their living. The second point to notice is that a poem rarely has the room to spell everything out, to state everything. That means that it has to work by suggesting events or moods, which it often does by using imagery – pictures or sounds which suggest more than they state. There are also times when a poem leaves a gap for us to complete. In

Arthur Waley's translation of an old Chinese poem called *Plucking the Rushes* we are told of a boy and girl who go out to pluck rushes for thatching in the village. The poems starts with an image:

> Green rushes with red shoots

This is an example of a picture which suggests more than it states – implication that this is Spring and an assumption that we will put Boy + Girl + Spring together. So, when they go out in a boat together, it is no surprise that, while they left at dawn to pick rushes, they rested under some trees until noon. Then come the lines

> You and I plucking rushes
> Had not plucked a handful when night came!

This is an example of the poem having a gap in it – whatever happened from noon till night is not described at all. The poet's artifice leaves us room to enter the poem from the statements and suggestions it has made so far, to weave these together with our own experience of life – and as a result, perhaps, to smile a half envious smile at the characters in the poem and a genially collusive smile with the poet about what he had created and how he has created it. In responding to what we have generated from the poem – our feelings about this Spring flirtation – we have also responded to how the poem helped to bring this about.

So far, then, we can talk of succinctness, of words being used to suggest more than they state, of matters being left unsaid. There is one other feature which a poem's brevity can bring about – what may be called 'virtual simultaneity'. Most poems are brief enough to be printed intact on a single page. We may read a poem line by line when we first meet it, but we are aware of the lines above and below the one we are currently looking at, and having read a poem we are very likely to keep some hold on all of it, at least visually. Look at this brief Victorian poem *A Memory* by William Allingham.

> Four ducks on a pond.
> A grass-bank beyond;
> A blue sky of spring,
> White clouds on the wing:

These first four lines, each with a picture which is related to the others, establish, by statement and implication, the colour, season and, probably, mood of the inhabitants of the poem, and of the speaker of the poem. Most pupils see both as being happy. Read on.

> What a little thing
> To remember for years –

Suddenly the poem shifts: we are now dealing with a precious memory. If we read the poem again, these two lines are present, on the page and in the sympathetic mind, interacting with the first four and affecting our response to them. But the poem has one more line.

> To remember with tears!

The poem has shifted again. Whatever the reason for the sorrow – what a gap Allingham has left for us to conjecture in – we cannot go back to those first four lines in any simple happiness. The last line is present alongside the first; all the lines are acting upon us at once – hence the concept of 'virtual simultaneity'. Novels expect us to 'read backwards and sideways' as well as forwards – to recall episodes and see their significance. Poetry does this much, much more. It is as if we are looking at an unrolled tapestry, at a woven pattern. As it is unrolled, so our understanding of its potential pattern changes, and each time we return, the pattern changes yet again. Another image we might use to describe a poem is an ice crystal, with its facets symmetrically balanced, their relationships, tensions and perspectives all contributing to the whole. In this analogy, the reader can look at the crystal at a fairly simple level – or can place it under a magnifying glass and observe it with detachment, while at the same time being involved in it and affected by it.

The more we can encourage pupils to dwell with a text and explore it, the more likely they are to be prepared to look at such effects as these. No violence is done to a poem by 'unrolling' it, provided that teacher and pupils celebrate it in the end by reading it as a complete entity.

1. Unrolling a poem

The technique, as exemplified by the Allingham poem, can be operated in the classroom by writing a fairly brief poem on an overhead projector transparency. Work out its phases and the points where they change. Cover up all the poem except for its first phase and ask for comments on what is happening so far: what is being stated, what is being suggested. Move on, phase by phase, each time asking what the pupils have found that is new; how the new phase is affected by, and how it affects, what has gone before. This is a simple approach, but it can be an effective one. It can be adapted for group work by writing out each phase on cards or on a computer disc. Some senior pupils will produce their own 'unrolling' games for the class to explore. Finally, if pupils are given a copy of a poem which has been printed at the centre of a fairly large sheet of paper, they can work collaboratively on linking items, to show their interplay. Using coloured pens, they can underline images which link; echoes of sounds; significant statements, implications or gaps; how a late line affects an early one – and so on.

2. Choosing a name

It is interesting how few pupils look at a poem's title, if it has one. It can sometimes be useful to keep the title secret for a while. Once the poem has been 'unrolled' you can ask pairs to think of what the poem might be called, so that its label fits the poem's contents and mood. It can be worth discussing the results to see how people have arrived at their various views of the poem. That can lead people to look at it again, to see what it was in the poem and in their make-up that caused them to share or differ in their perspectives. Henry Treece's ironically titled *Conquerors*, for instance, is likely to gain a range of powerful but unironic headings. William Blake's *Poison Tree* tends to earn such titles as *Hate* or *My Friend*. It is rare that the poet's title coincides with the pupils'. Discussing the differences can lead back into the poem yet again.

Breaking the pattern

1. Sequencing

'Unrolling' aims to do as little violence to a poem as possible, by approximating to the way that people actually read poems. To some teachers, 'sequencing' is more debatable. The technique is quite simple. A poem is sliced up into single lines, and pairs of pupils try to work out the original poem. This 'jigsaw puzzle' approach can certainly create considerable discussion about a poem's structure and intended sequence. It promotes awareness of prosodic features, such as rhythm, rhyme and layout, and of aspects of grammatical vocabulary. More important is an awareness of the thinking and feeling which drive the poem forward. A hymn or a lyric can be useful here, since verses may appear to be self-sufficient, but there are normally clues in the text as to which one should appear where in the overall structure.

2. Deletion

Traditional 'cloze' technique, with its deletion of every seventh word in a text, is probably over-used in some schools and some teachers dislike its temporary mutilation of a poem. Nevertheless, it can have certain virtues. For a start, a poem with gaps in it signals that it needs the active help of the reader. It is not seen as some tablet of stone handed down by a secular priest. It asks pupils to be constructively critical and to respond to all the features of a poem, in order to suggest the means of completing what has been removed. It encourages pupils to become much more aware of the fact that a poet, as a craftsperson, is faced with dilemmas and has choices to make.

The most frequent approach is to present a poem with significant words omitted completely or placed out of sequence as a list at the bottom of the poem. Pupils are asked to collaborate in filling the gaps by choosing words which fit the meaning, rhythm and rhyme of the poem. The technique can be more flexible than this. For instance, it is possible to omit words and phrases which contribute to a poem's mood. See the adjectives in Treece's *Conquerors* (Appendix 1a), for example. If a poem relies on a set of images, these can be deleted – to fill such gaps is a challenging task for senior pupils. In such instances, they can seek not only to replace what has been omitted but can go on to discuss what sort of dynamic has been restored to the poem by their contributions – what sort of imagery, what sort of mood, and so on. In these circumstances, collaborative learning has a focus and promotes 'conferring about' rather than simple 'conferring among'. It sets out to promote intellectual rigour through genuine problem-solving, rather than the flaccid shared ignorance which can sometimes result from poorly devised group work.

'Cloze' can be used for collaborative and individual reflection. It is always important to encourage a valuing of pupils' contributions to a poem. There will be occasions when they prefer their words, phrases or images to the poet's. This is ideal in helping them to discuss the original poem with respect rather than reverence and in showing them that they too have skills in choosing language for complex purposes.

3. Word options

An alternative to cloze is to print a poem with options at key points. For example, here are the first four lines of Thomas Hardy's bitter *I Look Into My Glass*, a poem of twelve short lines, with options built in:

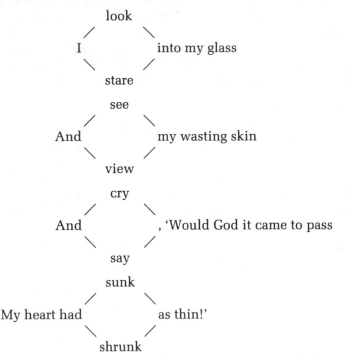

Choose a brief poem such as this, providing options at various points. Ask pairs to decide which options they wish to choose and to give their reasons. This is a fairly economical exercise in becoming aware of how a poet chooses words as part of her or his artifice. It is less of a hide-and-seek guessing game than cloze and some teachers feel that this approach is more faithful to the poet's endeavour in deciding the language of a poem.

Seeing the pattern

1. Pairings

Hardy's poem is ideal material for use with the technique of pairing – bringing together two poems which are connected, perhaps by a common theme. Looking in the mirror is a familiar theme in literature, from the Wicked Queen's 'Mirror, mirror on the wall, who is the fairest one of all?' onwards. Philip Larkin's poem *Skin* would make an excellent companion for Hardy's poem. While both poems explore and express the sadness of ageing through the image of looking into a mirror, Hardy's bitterness and anger are very different in tone from Larkin's wryness as he talks about his 'obedient daily dress'. Senior pupils could compare these poems' language and structure and their consequent mood and effect.

Pairing has a long established place in developing awareness of artifact. The psychologist Bruner has talked of 'contrastive learning' as a particularly fruitful approach in active learning. Another pairing, of *Conquerors* and *The Enemies*, is exemplified in Appendix 1a. Many pupils enjoy finding their own pairings, and it is interesting to see what it is that prompts them to link two poems. At its simplest, they are likely to find poems on the same material subject, such as cats, but others will progress to finding poems which are thematically linked. More mature students will find poems which are linked through their contrasting, rather than their similar, treatment of topic and mood.

2. Making choices

'Contrastive learning', the technique of comparing two items to see where similarities and dissimilarities lie, is a device English teachers often use. It might be used with two poems on a similar topic, or with a picture and a poem, to see what each has to say about the other. The same approach can be used by committing minor violence to a poem while at the same time holding the original in the reader's attention. Take, for example, Shelley's famous *Ozymandias*, a poem which remains widely read. The first few lines of the original run:

> I met a traveller from an antique land
> Who said: 'Two vast and trunkless legs of stone
> Stand in the desert . . . Near them, on the sand,
> Half sunk, a shattered visage lies, whose frown,
> And wrinkled lip, and sneer of cold command,
> Tell that its sculptor well those passions read . . .

It does not take long to work out some alterations, affecting rhyme, rhythm, or basic meanings; they can be fairly subtle or rather obvious. Imagine a version which started:

> I met a traveller from an ancient land
> Who said: 'Two huge and trunkless legs of stone.

These are fairly subtle vocabulary changes: not everyone might agree about which version of these lines was the original – or the better.

> Stick in the desert ... Near them, on the ground,

This is a little more obvious and pupils should be able to feel that there is more than one reason for being uneasy about 'ground'.

> Half sunk, a broken up visage lies, whose frown

This should raise eyebrows about an inappropriately modern idiom and about rhythm. And so the reading can go on.

   Another way of using this material is to produce two versions of the poem so that they appear in parallel. Include genuine lines in both. The last six lines of *Ozymandias* might look like this:

> And on the pedestal these words appear:
> 'Ozymandias, my name is, king of kings:
> Look on my creations, you Mighty, and despair.'
> Nothing beside remains. Round the decay
> Of that giant wreckage, boundless and deserted
> The lone and level sands stretch far away.

A second version might run:

> And on the pedestal this pride appears:
> 'My name is Ozymandias, king of kings:
> Look on my works, ye Mighty, and despair!'
> Nothing else is left. Around the decay
> Of that colossal wreck, boundless and bare
> The lonely, flattened sands stretch far away.

Senior readers can work together, to assemble their version of the original poem. One version of each line is Shelley's; the other is not. Making comparisons across the two poems and beginning to understand their patterns of thought and feeling, rhyme and rhythm, image and vocabulary, most groups manage to agree on about two-thirds of the poem. The important point is not whether they 'get the poem right' but whether their discussion promotes genuine exploration of the poem and raises awareness of it as artifact. When the workshop has made its decision, celebrate the poem with good readings of the original out loud. (The unofficial version might enjoy an airing as well!)

This device can appeal to the more subtle parodists in a senior group who can be encouraged to produce further versions of other poems to set as a challenge for other groups to re-assemble. In particular, it can lead to a detailed discussion about whether absolute synonyms exist and about the interplay of denotation and connotation – the literal meanings of words and their over- and undertones – in the structured language of a poem.

3.   Restoring the pattern

An old trick for getting pupils to see that a poet plays visual games is to show them 'shape' poems. From George Herbert's devotional poem *Easter Wings* to the sort of poems which no doubt most pupils in junior school will have written, such as cat poems in the outline of a cat – shape poetry will be familiar. But more conventional poems also signal something about themselves by their shapes. A handy technique is to advise pupils to look at a poem with eyes half closed so that they are aware of its outline, not its words. They can see, for example, if it is in one block or in three or four shorter ones, implying that thought is being 'paragraphed' in verses. They can see if the lines are long, implying, perhaps, a slow pace which might be to do with dignity, stateliness or weariness. They can see if the lines are particularly short, signalling energy of some kind – perhaps restlessness, brittleness or jokiness.

Following on from this, pupils can try repatterning into its original layout a poem which has been set out as prose. Younger ones may need to have a poem which has pretty obvious rhythm and rhyme clues about its original form. Older pupils should be encouraged to collaborate in trying to re-form a poem which has less obvious structure, before comparing their results with the original.

All of these approaches aim to encourage interest in a poem's artifice without losing its opportunity to affect the reader. They also try to encourage pupils to see that 'a poem' is in actual fact an event which they have helped to create – a moment when they interact with a code left by somebody else. The issue of poem as artifact can be approached by other routes, as earlier chapters have shown. When pupils draw their visual interpretation of a poem, they can be asked what it is in the poem which has helped to bring about that response. When they write a story suggested by a poem, they can be asked what the poem said and how it said it which helped to create that tale, and so on.

4.   Ante-Pastiche

The previous chapter suggested that pupils will gain some understanding of poetry as artifact by trying to write within conventional forms, from the haiku to the sonnet. It was also suggested that pastiche has a part to play. Ante-pastiche is an approach for use with seniors, perhaps of fifteen upwards, who set out to produce a poem by working collaboratively.

The technique is rather like a lesson in cookery, with the teacher providing the ingredients and the cooking instructions. These can be produced on a printed hand-out, but there is much to be said for issuing them 'live', for you can then suggest something of the mood and the tone of the poem as well. For example, introducing a Hardy poem (without mentioning his name) can go like this. 'You see a man walking in silence, slowly, behind a horse-drawn harrow – that's like a giant rake used for crumbling the soil after it's been ploughed and for tugging out the roots of couch-grass, which is a curse on any soil. The horse is old and stumbles along, and it's as if the man and the horse are both half-sleep. And you see the couch-grass has been heaped up here and there and been set fire to – but all that comes from it is a thin line of smoke, no flame. And yet the thought strikes you that this activity will continue even though whole lines of kings and queens come and go. And then you see a girl and her lover who come walking past, whispering to one another – and the thought strikes you that such love as theirs is likely to last longer than the whole history of wars. O.K? Those are the ingredients. I want the man and his horse in the first verse, the burning of the couch grass and your thoughts about the changelessness of such a scene and the passing of kings and queens in the second, and the rest of the ingredients in the third. If you can, work to a rhyme scheme of *abab, cdcd, efef*. If you really want to be clever, go for short lines, a lot of slow, monosyllabic words and single rhyme.'

That may sound daunting, but many lower sixth formers have found this workshop approach of producing their own poems first effective as a gateway to studying Thomas Hardy. Here are two first verses:

> Old man, old horse plod on together,
> Half-asleep across the soil,
> Oblivious of the winter weather,
> Wearied by their dreary toil.

> Across the ploughed earth they go,
> Man and horse bound as one,
> Minds and bodies tired and slow,
> Working till the setting sun.

It is important that the pupils' poems are duplicated and used for discussion about how they have grappled with issues of content and form before they meet the 'official' poem – so that when they encounter it, they have ideas of their own to trade with Hardy's *In Time of 'The Breaking of Nations'*.

> Only a man harrowing clods
>   In a slow silent walk
> With an old horse that stumbles and nods
> Half asleep as they stalk

They can look at the decisions which they made and compare them with those of the original – sometimes preferring their own, sometimes acceding to Hardy's superiority; sometimes accepting the focus that he chooses and sometimes arguing for the one that they have chosen instead. (It is interesting to note how few pupils come anywhere near the deliberate absence of punctuation in that first verse, for example, with its imaging of the unceasing to-and-fro harrowing of the field.) This technique can be used time and again, preferably with fairly short poems. It is worth starting with poets who use language in a relatively familiar way. Bolder, more heroic or bardic poets are worth leaving till a little later, since to meet Ted Hughes or Dylan Thomas on a first encounter with this method can be rather daunting and even dispiriting.

(Incidentally, this is an instance where some groups find working on a word processor useful, since everyone in a group can see the screen and help produce the poem. The final effort is also ready for the publication that this approach requires. The only word of warning is that pupils should be asked to run off copies of any draft stages, so that they can work on these as well, if necessary.)

Inviting questions – three approaches

The following three approaches are offered as examples of ways of generating discussion about poems with senior pupils – one is suggested by a poet, one by a teacher and one by a researcher.

1.   Versions – Oliver Bernard

Oliver Bernard is a British poet and is nationally recognised for his talent in speaking poetry. The technique described here is simple and elegant in the way it requires students to respond to a poem and its artifice.

Phase 1. Everyone is given a few minutes to read a poem through and to annotate it, so that it becomes a reading script.

Phase 2. Each person reads the poem to the other members of the group. At the end of each person's reading, the others in the group are required to say what they liked about it. 'I liked the bit where you put in that long pause, because ...' 'I liked the way that your voice went quiet at the end, because ...'. So the group hears the poem several times and becomes aware of the opportunity it offers for interpretation, just as a musical score or a play script is an opportunity for text and 'reader' to interact.

Phase 3. From its readings, the group works out its ideal, composite interpretation of the poem and chooses the best voice in the group for that particular poem.

Phase 4. The group trains that person, rehearsing the reading and adjusting it, until it is what the group wants it to be.

Matters can be left at that. Confident pupils, however, can take it further.

Phase 5. Each group's reader can celebrate the poem out loud to the class, which should be under the same obligation of identifying what it likes about each interpretation. After each reading, the 'trainers' – not the reader – can be asked to explain why they wanted the poem read in that way. Where groups produce different readings, you have the basis for further discussion on what it was in the poem, and in the readers' and trainers' skills, attitudes and histories, that allowed or encouraged this diversity. Such sessions rarely end in agreement and therefore may need careful, supportive handling. What they achieve, ideally, is an awareness that poetry is never fixed or finite; that it uses artifice and its own choice of rules to create a 'form' in which it can remain at least partly elusive and free; and that we should be glad that its artifice makes it so.

2. Asking questions

Penny Blackie's article on this topic in the journal of the National Association for the Teaching of English (*English in Education* 5, 3) profoundly affected many other teachers' approaches to poetry.

It could be said that a poem asks questions rather than gives answers. In that case, it seems sensible to ask questions back! Penny Blackie's approach asks pupils to pose the questions which they feel are necessary. Many of their questions will not be to do directly with a poem as artifact; but discussion of them will inevitably deal with that topic.

Phase 1. Pupils are asked to read a poem which is going to be the object of later discussion, and to write down anything which strikes them about it – comments about a pleasing line, a puzzling image, an unknown word, a general reaction. The only rule is that all comments must be written as questions.

Phase 2. These jottings are collected in and used to work out an agenda of issues for the lesson. Both participants have some knowledge from which to start: the pupils of the poem and the teacher of their initial responses to it.

Having to jot down responses as questions is important. It enables students to slip in genuine questions which they might feel embarrassed to ask. For example, in the poem *Timothy Winters* by Charles Causley, we are told that a young boy's drunken grandmother 'sits in the grate with a gin'. It has been disconcerting to find how many thirteen year olds have jotted down 'What is a grate?' as a genuine question. Central heating has a lot to answer for! The technique also encourages pupils to jot down things that they already know, thus giving them a chance to be confident in the classroom.

Perhaps most important of all is the fact that intuitions are called into question. The boy who loved the phrase 'green tigering the gold' in Ted Hughes's poem *Pike* jotted down 'Why do I like "green tigering the gold"?' The student who found a poem by Robert Frost boring had to rephrase his usual closure remark 'It's boring!', into the access remark 'Why is this poem boring?' That led to discussion not only of that poem but of poetry in general. With the question mark, any item of response has potential as a topic for discussion. It is interesting how often questions have their origin in difficulty over comprehending the 'special' language that a poet has chosen to use – her or his vocabulary, syntax, layout, imagery, succinctness, use of suggestion and gaps – and so on. Using Penny Blackie's approach, the teacher can identify topics for discussion which grow out of the pupils' pre-occupations and ensure that they include some thought about the poem itself.

Penny Blackie's approach leads to the teacher finally editing and control-ling the agenda of the pupils' questions. There is every reason for encour-aging pupils who are familiar with group work to create their own agenda from the jottings that they have made, using them to identify issues for discussion within the group before presenting the most important ones to other groups or to the whole class.

3. Forming views – Patrick Dias

The approaches outlined in much of this book have been based on the premise that people learn about poetry by making it, reading it and reflecting upon it as naturally and as frequently as possible. That means that there will be a great deal of incidental talk – what has been called 'gossip' – as pupils simply browse for poems to read together in a quiet half hour or as they work out how to storyboard a film script of a poem or engage in many of the other activities presented here and elsewhere.

Patrick Dias (the Director of the International Poetry Response Project, based at McGill University, Montreal) has produced a slightly more forma-lised procedure for pupils to work with. It has a set of 'rules' which enable and require everyone in a group to assume a set of necessary tactics in exploring a poem through talk.

Phase 1. Pupils get together in small groups: four is a usual size. Each of them has a copy of the poem to be discussed. The poems are often provided by a researcher or teacher, but the technique works equally well with poems provided by pupils themselves. The group has time in which to read the poem quietly, each member working out how she or he will read the poem to the others.

Phase 2. Each pupil reads the poem to the group. The readings can follow on from one another with Phase 3 starting at the end of the whole series of readings, or a group can decide to interleave Phase 3 between each reading.

Phase 3. This phase is intended to set up reflective discussion about individual and collaborative response. Take, for example, a group which decides to complete all its readings before going on to the discussion phase. The readings are completed. The first reader makes a comment about the poem and his or her response to it. It can be presented as a statement or a question and be about the whole poem or part of it. Each person in the group is expected to build on that contribution. They can take their time and choose how they want to do so – perhaps by answering a point, or referring to something in the poem, or asking a question which is relevant to that contributor's initiating comment. The important point is that everyone is engaged in developing further insight into the poem and into response. Once the round is completed, the next person proffers a comment and the others contribute to it; and so the process continues, until everyone has started a brief discussion by offering an item of personal response and has responded to everyone else's starting points.

Phase 4. After this, a group can move into more naturalistic, free-ranging discussion, if it wishes. Some groups prefer to use the ritualised discussion more than once before branching out and might even return to it in the middle of an open discussion, if they find themselves in some sort of difficulty.

Initially, groups may be a little self-conscious about this approach, but it is interesting to see how many groups will choose this one out of their range of approaches, if they are given an option about how to tackle a poem. It provides security in that everyone adopts several necessary and active roles, as a reader of a poem and a listener to it, and as a speaker and a listener in the following exploratory discussion. The technique is made more effective if the group uses a tape recorder. It is interesting how its presence helps to focus a group and how often the group will seek out something that it said earlier in the discussion, in order to clarify, dispute or reinforce a current point. The tape-recorder becomes a silent, tactful secretary which reads back its notes to the group on demand, so that the group can reflect upon its own response. Recordings can also be useful if you wish to explore for yourself how your pupils work together in responding to a poem.

Dias's technique, as presented here, ends at its fourth phase. It is worth noting that there are times when a fifth phase is justified. The pupils have had their say, working individually first, then through groups of increasing size to plenary discussion of their views and their insights. They have been able to collaborate in the key enterprise of 'occupying the middle ground'. That may well suffice on many occasions. But there will be occasions when the other person in the room, the teacher, may have things to say about the poem and his or her perceptions of it and responses to it. To deny these is to create a false silence. The teacher has things to say by virtue of sheer life-experience as well as academic ability. Provided that what he or she has to say is offered modestly, tentatively and in forms which create further thought on the part of the pupils, the teacher is not only entitled to speak but is obliged to. Often, comment can be couched in the form of questions which promote further reflection and perhaps offer divergence rather than some 'correct' answer; and it can often be expressed by picking up the pupils' own insights for further development. Sometimes, there is room for a teacher's brief display of enthusiasm, commitment and sheer knowledge, to bear witness to being personally moved by a poem. That may need to be rare, in order to avoid dominance. It need not be extinct.

Looking and listening

There are many other ways into creating an awareness of poem as artifact, and much of this book has been devoted to introducing them. For example, a guided reading approach was suggested in Chapter 4, and in Chapter 6 it was suggested that hearing a poet read his or her own poetry, preferably live but otherwise on a record, could lead to a sense of a poem's shape in action.

Whatever devices your pupils find most useful in their journeys of exploration, there is a place for the occasional guided tour. Some colleagues would argue that these are morally wrong and educationally unjustified. We do not agree. We would certainly agree that it is not the teacher's job to marshall pupil's thinking about every poem or to provide pre-packaged, safe notes which they ingest and regurgitate for some dead form of testing. That sort of well-intentioned tyranny is not to be defended. But there are occasions when seeing and hearing an adult in action, interacting with a poem, can be as elegant and exciting and *moving* as seeing and hearing a musician play a piece of music and explaining why it was interpreted in that way. In other words, there are occasions when pupils, especially at senior level, may be moved positively by listening to a poet or a scholar read and explore out loud what can be found in and what can be created from the poem.

At its best, this approach should develop in a climate where your pupils feel confident enough to accept the invitation to discuss their response with the person they have been listening to by asking questions and by giving their views on the poem. To impose adult perceptions cannot be justified; neither can denying access to them. We are all in the business of exploring poetry together, talking and listening to one another and to the voices that our encounters with poems create. If pupils can see how tentative we are, how exploratory, how insecure and provisional – and can see that this is part of the excitement – perhaps they will be prepared for becoming the 'creative partner' that the Canadian novelist W.O. Mitchell talks of, who 'reads through a sort of minefield' in which the poet's words are the triggers for a *reader* to 'set off explosions of recognition'.

If this brief book serves to promote that collaboration, then it will have succeeded in its aim.

Appendix 1a: Poems that work

Throughout this book we have argued that pupils should be given every opportunity to find the poetry they want to explore and should often be given the choice of how they want to explore those poems. But that doesn't mean that teachers shouldn't have enthusiasms, and there are occasions when the teacher will judge it right to introduce a poem or a cluster of poems instead.

There is a simple technique to help the teacher keep records of poems which he or she proposes to use at some time. Each poem's record has three components:
– a copy of the poem
– the teacher's own reactions to the poem
– the teacher's general ideas about what approaches might help when it is introduced to pupils.

It might be handy to produce a three-part form on which to record the poem and jot down responses and ideas, in order to build up a standardised folder. That can then be adopted as a way of working across the department, with poems and ideas being kept in departmental files for colleagues to share and develop. Extra sheets on further teaching approaches can be clipped to a poem as other colleagues use it and the original teaching ideas.

If a departmental collection is produced, there needs to be a filing system. Small personal collections of poems are easily filed in alphabetical order of title, for instance, but that approach will not suffice with a bigger collection which is to be used by several people.

The small sample of poems presented here is not intended to be taken as some sort of guide as to what makes 'good poetry'. It contains a few poems that two teachers have found many 14 year-olds and upwards have enjoyed exploring more deeply. They are presented here in order to show how the system of making notes works for them. The system can be adopted and adapted to suit the needs and interests of individual teachers and pupils.

From the Navajo Beautyway Healing Chart

adapted by M. J. Hayhoe

All that has harmed me will leave me,
    leaving my body cool once more.
Within me today, I shall be well.
All fever will come from me
    and leave me, leave my brow cool.
I will hear today
    and see to day
    and be my own true self today.
This is the day that I shall walk.
This is the day when all that is ill will leave me
    and I shall be as I was
    as I walk in a cool body.
This day onwards I shall be happy
    for nothing will prevent me.
I shall walk and Beauty will go before me
I shall walk and Beauty will be behind me
I shall walk and Beauty will be above me.
I shall walk and Beauty will be beneath me.
I shall walk and Beauty will surround me.
I shall walk and speak of Beauty.
For the rest of my days I shall be whole.
    for all things are Beautiful.

Comments

1. **Content and mood**: Navajo healing chant – beautiful incantatory verse, a mixture of faith and wishing
2. **Structure and approach**: in translation, a free verse poem – but with patterning provided by repetition of key words and phrases. Note the powerful six lines of repetition in the 'I shall walk' series, with the variation at the end of each line moving from being physically well to bearing witness to Beauty.
3. **Language**: very simple vocabulary – a few key words related to being unwell physically and spiritually, and then further key words to celebrate the ideal state of physical and spiritual wholeness.
4. **Further comment**: a sound poem rather than a visual one – and also a touch poem with its sense of coolness and implied fever, and in the sense of being in touch with the surrounding force of Beauty.

Possibilities

Maybe a poem for dramatisation, if handled carefully.
    A poem for class or group reading, to try to capture its strands of faith and

wishing. This poem could be an example of quiet, provided for contrast with *The Blacksmiths*, with its frenetic heat and noise.

This could be a poem for pairs to produce abstract sketches from, rather than realistic pictures. They could then go on to discuss what they find in one another's pictures and link their perceptions to a discussion of the healing chant.

This is an example of verse which depends on repetition – a strong stylistic feature in many oral traditions. Senior pupils could seek further examples of this, e.g. The Beatitudes in St. Matthew, Chapter 5, or the Fire Sermon of Buddha and discuss how such poetic devices enhance the rhetorical effect the speakers are seeking.

Another version of the Healing Chant is to be found in *The Rattle Bag*, edited by Seamus Heaney and Ted Hughes, under the title 'In beauty may I walk'. Pupils could compare the two chants and see what they have in common; where their content differs; how they are similar or different in mood. Groups could adopt one of the two poems and argue its case by preparing a reading of it; by preparing an illustration for it; or by preparing a tableau or mime for it (if the class has this self-confidence and maturity).

Seniors could seek charms, wishes, healing songs, curses from other oral traditions (Old English, Inuit, African, etc.), or could investigate other such poetry in translation from other Amerindian peoples. This could lead to two discussions, one on whether such 'verse with a purpose' can be called poetry and the other on whether translations are successful as poems in their own right.

The Blacksmiths
Poet unknown

> Swarte smekyd smethes smateryd wyth smoke
> Dryve me to deth wyth den of here dyntes.
> Swech noys on nyghtes ne herd men never:
> What knavene cry and clateryng of knockes!
> The cammede congons cryen after 'col! col!'
> And blowen there bellewys, that al here brayn brestes.
> 'Huf, puf!' seith that on. 'Haf, paf!' that other.
> Thei spyttyn and spraulyn and spellen many spelles.
> They gnauen and gnacchen, thei gronys togydere
> And holdyn hem hote wyth here hard hamers.
> Of a bole-hyde ben here barm-fellys.
> Here schankes ben schakeled for the fere-flunderys.
> Hevy hamerys thei han, that hard ben handled,
> Stark strokes thei stryken on a stelyd stokke:
> Lus, bus! Las, das! rowtyn be rowe.
> Sweche dolful a dreme the devyl it todryve!

The mayster logith a lityl and lasceth a lesse,
Twyneth hem tweyn, and towchith a treble:
Tik, tak! hic, hac! tiket, taket! tyk tak!
Lus, bus! lus, das! swych lyf thei ledyn
All clothemerys. Cryst hem gyve sorwe!
May no man for brenwaterys on nyght han hys rest!

Smoke-blackened smiths smattered with smoke
Drive me to death with the din of their hammering.
Such noise in the night no man heard ever:
What calling out by servants, what clattering blows!
The snub-nosed changelings call for 'Coal! Coal!'
And blow their bellows till their brains burst.
'Huff, puff,' goos that one and 'Haff, paff!' another.
They spit and sprawl and never stop chattering.
They grind and gnash their teeth, they groan together
All of a sweat with their hard working hammers.
Bull-hides are what their leather aprons are made from.
Their shanks are protected against fiery sparks.
They have heavy hammers that they handle powerfully,
Striking stark strokes on a steel anvil:
'Lus, bus! Las, das!' they beat out in turn.
Such a dreadful din would destroy the Devil!
The master lengthens a short piece of iron, hammers a shorter,
Twines them together and strikes a treble note.
'Tik, tak! Hic, hac! Tiket, taket! Tyk, tak!
'Lus, bus! Lus, das!' Such is the life they lead.
All mare-tailors. May Christ make them wretched!
No man, with those water-burners, can get his night's rest!

(translated by M. J. Hayhoe)

Comments

1. **Content and mood:** spirited Fourteenth Centry poem! Is this the first
   tirade against noise pollution in English? If it is, the poet writes with
   zestful anger and an eye and ear for detail which suggest he knows what
   he's complaining about!
2. **Structure and approach:** a long, long-lined poem which hammers away
   at the reader – very much intended to be a tape-recording of the
   blacksmith's 'next door', so that the reader experiences much of what
   the speaker is complaining about. But it's also very visual, full of detail
   and non-stop action, almost like a speeded-up early Hollywood comedy.
3. **Language:** very much a sound poem; so look at the extensive onomatopoeia. It is also a poem depending on front-rhyme (alliteration) which
   makes for a much more punchy, declamatory poem – it takes a lot of

energy to read extensive alliteration such as this. Note the spelling changes and the unfamiliar vocabulary.

4. **Further comment**: curiously contemporary poem in its concern with a topic of our own times and in the 'Dear Sir ... Yours disgustedly' energy of it all.

Possibilities

Excellent for drama, maybe first as a mime (see also Chapter 7) and then building on layers of sound – the sound effects of the smithing processes; the confusion of the workers' voices; the voice-over of the poem itself. (Splendid occasion for a great deal of legitimate row, but it will have to be done in a proper drama area or when there isn't another class near!)

Also good for groups to work up as a sound tape i.e. as above but without the improvised drama.

Produce an alliteratively abusive poetic riposte from the blacksmiths to this complaint against the productivity drive of a proud British industry.

Produce an alliterative poem which describes the first night after the smithy has burned down and all is silent and still.

Get groups to produce the poem as a cartoon strip or as a set for a cartoon film, using only four colours which they think appropriate to the poem.

Get groups to look for other poems which have a lot of noise in them, to discuss their presentation, perhaps along Oliver Bernard lines (see p. 117), and to present the poems with an explanation of what purposes the noise serves.

Get groups to find the quietest poem that they can and present it as a contrast, with an explanation on why the poem is so quiet – serenity, grief, mystery, fear, contemplation?

Conquerors
Henry Treece

> By sundown we came to a hidden village
> Where all the air was still
> And no sound met our tired ears, save
> For the sorry drip of rain from blackened trees
> And the melancholy song of swinging gates.
> Then through a broken pane some of us saw
> A dead bird in a rusting cage, still
> Pressing his thin tattered breast against the bars,
> His beak wide open. And
> As we hurried through the weed-grown street,
> A gaunt dog started up from some dark place
> And shambled off on legs as thin as sticks
> Into the wood, to die at least in peace.

No one had told us victory was like this;
Not one amongst us would have eaten bread
Before he'd filled the mouth of the grey child
That sprawled, stiff as a stone, before the shattered door.
There was not one who did not think of home.

Comments

1. **Content and mood:** depressing poem about effects of war. Implicit moral message.
2. **Structure and approach:** simple continuous narrative in order to take the reader without stopping through a desolate scene – a bit like a movie.

    'Visual' rather than 'sound' based – strong sense of silence (nobody talks) – sense of wariness and weariness.

    Description written as a series of tableaux. Note how these 'pictures' are also images, i.e. they summon up more than the visual in the mind – they start with a foreign (?) countryside, go into a village, and then focus on creatures of increasing value in a human community – pet bird, dog, child – leading to thoughts of the invaders' own homes.
3. **Language:** most of the nouns are to do with life and good things – a settlement and some of its creatures. These are sabotaged by the absence of the rightful adult carers and the presence of the invaders – also sabotaged on the page by their adjectives, which are all to do with destruction and dread and death. Exhausted verbs – no dynamism, energy.

    Note the title – increasingly bitter as the poem is read – casts doubts over the whole poem and makes the reader go back to it at the end of the poem with a revised, sourly ironic (?) view.
4. **Further comments:** full of questions – Who are the 'we'? Where are the adults? What led up to this? What happens after that last line? All of these are the 'stories not told, the poems not stated'.

Possibilities

Pupils jot down their immediate responses to the poem before pooling them in small groups.

Ideal poem for producing a filmscript. If a VCR is available, this could be used to video aspects of the collage, with the poem read as a voice-over. Senior groups could keep a log of the process and write up a justification of what they did for coursework assessment. It could also be used as the focus for a collage of pictures – pupils' own or published pictures.

Tableaux – any chance of working with Art to produce a set of pictures?

Also surely a good chance for improvised drama – the poem has no dialogue, so it could be mimed as a first stage and/or groups could produce the event as a dialogue for live (or taped) presentation. (See also Chapter 7.)

Pupils to produce a reading which picks up this silence and unease – could pick up the 'we' of the poem as a series of voices. Could be done on tape. Could use sound effects/music, if they can justify it. (Links with music?)

Before meeting the poem, do some work on connotation – here, what an accumulation of nouns brings to mind – 'sundown' and 'village', then 'rain' and 'trees', then (pet) 'bird' and 'dog' and 'child' and 'home'. Aim for notions of life, community, affection, i.e. what the village used to be like. Then meet the poem – chance to do some work on how the nouns affect one another, and the subversion provided by the adjectives.

Either read the poem without the title and let groups invent their own – discuss results – or give the title and see what it summons up before going on to the poem. Handy chance to stress the occasional centrality of a title.

Pupils can opt to write a poem which takes someone along the village street in peacetime – perhaps describing the flight/destruction, writing the thoughts of individual soldiers or their letters home.

Chance to link this with other fiction and non-fiction on war – older pupils in discussion on war and consequences. Possible poems: W.H. Auden's *Embassy*; Dylan Thomas's 'The hand that signed the paper'; Arthur Waley's *The Little Cart*; Elizabeth Jennings' *The Invaders*.

Discussion at senior level on what is valued in peacetime, what in war-time, and why. Discussion on how far a poem with a moral can be a poem?

Flight of the Roller Coaster
Raymond Souster

> Once more around should do it, the man confided ...
>
> And sure enough, when the roller-coaster reached the peak
> Of the giant curve above me – screech of its wheels
> Almost drowned by the shriller cries of the riders—
>
> Instead of the dip and plunge with its landslide of screams
> It rose in the air like a movieland magic carpet, some
>   wonderful bird,
> And without fuss or fanfare swooped slowly across the
>   amusement park,
> Over Spook's Castle, ice-cream booths, shooting-gallery; and
>   losing no height
> Made the last yards above the beach, where the cucumber-cool
> Brakeman in the last seat saluted
> A lady about to change from her bathing-suit.
>
> Then, as many witnesses duly reported, headed leisurely over
>   the water,
> Disappearing mysteriously all too soon behind a low-lying
>   flight of clouds.

Comments

1. **Content and mood:** fantasy poem about a roller coaster breaking free and flying away. Mood is a mixture of floating away on the roller coaster, tinged with occasional humour – but it is possible to find an ambivalent, potentially disconcerting element as well.
2. **Structure and approach:** several brief sets of long lines which capture the gliding escape of the roller coaster, following a problematic first line and concluding with a stately final couple of lines. One line of dialogue starts the poem, followed by the noise of the ride – but then the poem becomes quiet and largely visual, contrasting the world which the roller coaster is leaving with its mysterious vanishing.
3. **Language:** quietly narrated – use of extended sentences which break through the ends of lines, just as the roller coaster breaks rules and goes free. The language contrasts sound and silence; the jumble of the fun-fair and beach with the elegant flight of the released roller coaster.
4. **Further comment:** Likely to be seen as a happy, literally escapist poem, especially by younger pupils. Senior pupils might be interested in looking more closely: Who is the man in the first line? Why does he 'confide'? With whom? Is he on the ground, like the 'I' of the poem – in the roller coaster – somewhere else? Why is there no reference to the reaction of the riders (apart from the brakeman) as it disappears?

Possibilities

Establish a context through pupils writing/discussing anecdotes related to their fantasising, wishes to escape, dreams about flying. Include anecdotes about fun-fairs, encounters with thrills, terrors, pleasures.

Exploit the visual – an ideal poem for younger pupils to produce a large-scale collage and then video with the poem as voice-over. Could also be used for a film script.

Use for choral verse – structure the reading to express the change from audio-visual to almost completely visual in the poem. Seniors could use the Oliver Bernard group rehearsal approach (see p. 117).

Use the Blackie 'asking questions' approach (see p. 118) to see what intrigues pupils. Maybe ask questions about the story which the poem hints at or doesn't even tell: who 'the man' might be, what has happened before the poem, and what might happen after.

Pupils to write other poems on fairground experiences – swings, hall of mirrors, ride of death, shooting gallery, etc.

Seniors to discuss how a poem could be created using real transport: underground train/school bus/holiday-trip aeroplane as the vehicle. Groups then to create their own poem (maybe using wordprocessor?), trying to achieve the tone/mood which they have perceived in Souster's poem.

Reading and discussion of 'escapes' in prose fantasy – the *Alice* books, the opening of Alan Garner's *Elidor*, etc.

Discussion on fantasy in poetry leading to each senior group producing an annotated compilation (print or tape) of ten poems which cover the range of topics and treatments that can be found, from the light-hearted and fatuous to the sinister or to the profoundly spiritual. Individuals to write up commentary from this as a coursework task.

The Garden of Love
William Blake

> I went to the Garden of Love,
> And saw what I never had seen:
> A Chapel was built in the midst,
> Where I used to play on the green.
>
> And the gates of this Chapel were shut,
> And 'Thou shalt not' writ over the door;
> So I turn'd to the Garden of Love
> That so many sweet flowers bore;
>
> And I saw it was filled with graves,
> And tomb-stones where flowers should be;
> And Priests in black gowns were walking their rounds,
> And binding with briars my joys & desires.

Comments

1. **Content and mood:** deceptively simple poem – seemingly a journey to a childhood play-place to which access is now denied, but obviously implies much more than its literal meaning.
2. **Structure and approach:** told as a brief tale in three verses – visually, a very regular structure but not to the ear – notice the run-on lines, and listen to the hammering of the last stanza, as the anger (?) builds up.
    This poem uses strong images and emblems. Some seem to stand for natural (and once upon a time innocent?) pleasures – others for forces (religion?) which have banned their revisitation?
3. **Language:** very powerful because it is kept so simple – lots of mono-syllabic words, which means lots of stressed words as well; simple rhyme scheme in the first two verses and naïve repetition, e.g. of 'Garden of Love' and of 'flowers'. The simple style suggests a simple narrator – but then comes that last verse, with the hammering repetition of 'And' at the start of every line and the crescendo of energy in the long last two lines with their internal rhymes. Note the two explicit colours and what they are linked to.
4. **Further comment:** disturbing poem! The language may look simple, but probably a poem for seniors.

Possibilities

Ideal poem for groups to ask questions about, following the Penny Blackie techniques (see p. 118). What are *their* questions about this poem? They could be used as Blackie would or groups could discuss their own questions.

Also suitable for an Oliver Bernard reading (see p. 117), to see if they find different moods in the poem – maybe not always anger but resignation, etc? Could use the interpretations for discussion.

Give the poem without its title and get pairs to decide on the title they'd want to give. Use their choices for discussion about the poem.

Ideal for producing a simple picture strip or a single picture, perhaps allowing only the colours explicit and implicit in the poem. (Could show them some Blake illustrations first – or after?)

If it's a class who are good at mime and not self-conscious about it, this could make a good mime or tableau series, with voice-over.

Search out, or create, music or sounds to go with the poem and discuss the choice.

Have groups look at the tale of the Garden of Eden in the Bible (Genesis, Chapters 2 and 3), and see if there are any links. Some might like to produce a serious pastiche of this poem, based on the story of the expulsion from Eden.

Commission groups to look at Blake's *Songs of Innocence and Experience* (and at their illustration?) with a view to further study.

I look into my glass
Thomas Hardy

> I look into my glass,
> And view my wasting skin,
> And say, 'Would God it came to pass
> My heart had shrunk as thin!'
>
> For then, I, undistrest
> By hearts grown cold to me.
> Could lonely wait my endless rest
> With equanimity.
>
> But Time, to make me grieve,
> Part steals, lets part abide;
> And shakes this fragile frame at eve
> With throbbings of noontide.

Comments

1. **Content and mood:** literally a reflective poem – the authorial 'persona' seeing the self reflected in a mirror and then reflecting on the passions which continue to inhabit the ageing body. Complex mood – melancholy, yes, but other emotions as well, depending on the reader, perhaps.

2. **Structure and approach:** three quatrains with the control of a rhyme and metrical scheme – but the reading works against the metronome, the feelings struggle against the decorum of the scheme.

3. **Language:** a lot of stark simplicity – every word in the first verse with the simple weight of a monosyllable, for instance. But this is deceptive (cf. Blake's *Garden of Love*) – in fact a carefully contrived poem, including vocabulary, e.g. why choose 'view' instead of 'see'? Because of the brevity and simplicity, a lot of the words have great power, e.g. some of the words in the last stanza.

4. **Further comment:** linguistically simple on the surface perhaps, but content suggests that this is a senior poem.

Possibilities

Good poem for groups to present alternative readings of. Could be a poem to issue without giving the sex of the poet and asking groups to use male reader and then female. Discussion on whether this poem applies to all people or to one sex.

Draw attention to the vocabulary's power by producing a version with alternative words at key points – view/see; muse/say; shrunk/grown, etc. Groups to discuss alternatives and their effects on the poem.

Discuss the bitter wish in lines 3 and 4; why the poem refers to God and then to Time – and other issues students wish to raise.

Seniors to work in groups and adopt another poem on ageing – one to look at Philip Larkin's *Skin*, one at W.B. Yeats's splendid late poem *Politics*, another to look at Jenny Joseph's *Warning*.

Essay on the theme of ageing in poetry.

In-a Brixtan Markit

James Berry

> I walk in-a Brixtan markit,
> believin I a respectable man,
> you know. An wha happn?
>
> Policeman come straight up
> and search mi bag!
> Man – straight to mi.
> Like them did a-wait fi mi.
> Come search mi bag, man.
>
> Fi mi bag!
> An wha them si in deh?
> Two piece a yam, a dasheen,
> a han a banana, a piece a pork
> an mi lates Bob Marley.

Man all a suddn I feel
mi head nah fi mi. This yah now
is when man kill somody, nah!

'Tony', I sey, 'hol on. Hol on,
Tony. Dohn shove. Dohn shove.
Dohn move neidda fis, tongue
nor emotion. Battn down, Tony.
Battn down.' An, man, Tony win.

Comments

1. **Content and mood:** poem in Caribbean English about a black Briton being stopped and searched in London and his fury, self-control and sense of victory.
2. **Structure and approach:** told as if the stopped person is confiding directly to the reader. Very much a 'sound' poem of uninterrupted, rapid monologue. Five irregular 'stanzas', one for each phase of the episode. Very short lines, which echo the energy of the narrator.
3. **Language:** written in Jamaican dialect. Raises the issue of how far spelling can convey not only pronunciation but the cadence of a dialect. Very few distinctive dialect words – worth comparing with other dialect poems?
4. **Further comment:** ambivalent poem – anger or triumph or both? Also a protest poem?

Possibilities

A poem likely to need a context. Start with sharing anecdotes about being stopped/about other people being stopped – perhaps old people stopped on suspicion of shop-lifting, people going through Customs, pupils being stopped by a teacher in their previous school. (Need to be careful – tales being told *not* to assign blame but to explore the feelings of the person stopped.)

Some could set the poem out as prose on a wordprocessor, to see how this affected the poem's interpretation – might hand the prose version on disc to other groups who haven't met the poem, to see what layout they give it and discuss why.

Occasion for desk-based drama as pupils work in pairs: *A* reading the poem spiritedly to *B*. *B* becoming the sympathetic 'you' of the poem; then *B* and *A* swap roles. This could lead to small groups rehearsing a mime version to be acted out alongside the poem or reworking the poem as a play script.

Poem's structure captures its speed and energy. Pupils to write the policeman's account of the episode and adjust layout to fit his pace and mood. Results to be made public and discussed?

Poem for reading out loud – maybe using the Oliver Bernard rehearsal approach (see p. 117).

Groups to rework the poem into Standard English and read their results out loud. Discussion on what has been transferred successfully and what has been lost in the process. Maybe reverse the process, with a poem in Standard English being reworked in whatever dialects are to be found in the area, with the same following discussion.

Look at poems in Caribbean and other ethnic dialects – younger pupils to browse in Morag Styles' *I like this stuff* and *You'll love this stuff* (Cambridge University Press), etc.; older ones to browse in Paula Burnett's *Penguin Book of Caribbean Verse*, etc. Senior pupils to look at poems in other dialects, e.g. Scots (Robert Burns), Dorset (William Barnes), etc. Records and tapes to be used wherever available.

Senior pupils to look at other poems of protest – Wole Soyinka's *Telephone Conversation*; protest poems of old (folk songs, street ballads, etc.) and current protest – various sources around the world (freedom movements, anti-pollution, etc.). Ideal contrast could be 'archy is shocked' in *archy and mehitabel* by don marquis – account of a man being stopped for eating his glass eye on a subway train and not restraining himself the way the narrator does in the Berry poem. Maybe further work on songs of protest, witty or serious, by other poets or by themselves.

With senior pupils, explore poetry chosen as a vehicle for protest. What sorts of poem? Why? To what effect?

The Enemies
Elizabeth Jennings

Last night they came across the river and
Entered the city. Women were awake
With lights and food. They entertained the band,
Not asking what the men had come to take
Or what strange tongue they spoke
Or why they came so suddenly through the land.

Now in the morning all the town is filled
With stories of the swift and dark invasion;
The women say that not one stranger told
A reason for his coming. The intrusion
Was not for devastation:
Peace is apparent still on hearth and field.

Yet all the city is a haunted place.
Man meeting man speaks cautiously. Old friends
Close up the candid looks upon their face.
There is no warmth in hands accepting hands;
Each ponders, 'Better hide myself in case
Those strangers have set up their homes in minds

I used to walk in. Better draw the blinds
Even if the strangers haunt in my own house.'

Comments

1. **Content and mood:** a mysterious and sombre poem which might relate to any invasion at any time and place in history or equally as a symbol it might relate to changing ideas and values.
2. **Structure and approach:** there is a strong pattern of half-rhyme throughout the poem, perhaps reflecting the meaning and its half-known facts, which do not quite connect one with another. The first two stanzas are of six lines, rhyming *ababba*. In the first stanza the third *b* rhyme is a half-rhyme. In the second stanza the *a* rhymes are a sequence of half-rhymes. The third stanza is longer, being of eight lines, and the added length perhaps gives added weight, and hence solemnity, to the meaning. The rhyme scheme in stanza three runs *abababba*, though this time it is the *b* rhymes which are all half-rhymed as a sequence, and the final line provides a striking half-rhyme with the preceding, regularly rhymed *a* lines.
3. **Language:** the viewpoint is that of someone who lives in the invaded town, and is recounting the events of the immediate past carefully, not revealing any emotion or personal opinion. The language is formal, not in modern idiom, which gives it a timeless quality. The vocabulary is simple, in contrast with the overall significance of the events. Images such as lights, food, hearth, field are simple concepts but profound in that they evoke universal human needs, so extending the cultural significance of the poem.

Possibilities

Part of the power of the poem is its understatement and what it leaves unsaid. This is an open door for active interpretation, to get inside the people involved – both invaders and invaded – to explore their true feelings. This makes it an excellent poem to use as a springboard for drama, and ideas for this are explored in Chapter 7.

It could form part of a study of invasions such as that of the Channel Islands during World War Two, or more recent invasions. Such a project might involve exploring documentary evidence in the form of film or archive accounts of passive resistance.

The poem links well with two other poems: Henry Treece's poem *Conquerors* and Arthur Waley's translation of Chen Tzu-Lung's *The Little Cart* both of which have a similar timeless quality. *Conquerors* is presented from the viewpoint of the invaders, though in a more destructive context. *The Little Cart* is from the viewpoint of the townspeople who have decided to flee. To study all three together as a cluster would encourage contrastive learning and, hopefully, deeper empathy into the human condition.

Creative writing could involve scripting the dialogue between the women and their families – whispered in corridors so that the soldiers cannot hear. Perhaps some do not agree with the urbane treatment given to the soldiers.

Townspeople and soldiers do not speak the same language. This might lead to exploring sign language communication. 'How would you show that you wanted to visit your grandparents' house on the other side of the city?' and so on.

Inventing a foreign language can be tedious, but creative writing might present an imagined dialogue of the soldiers on the left-hand page of an exercise book, and the townspeople's responses on the opposite page, to show incomprehension and misunderstanding throughout an interaction.

The two facing pages of an exercise book might be used to show 'before and after' conversations between 'old friends', with the 'before' dialogue on the left-hand page and the 'after' on the facing page.

Discussion might take the direction of problem-solving; if you were the Mayor of the town, what would you do? How might people communicate without arousing suspicion? If you were to write a letter (to be translated by the invaders) asking to be left alone, how would you best state your case?

In a Breath
Carl Sandburg

> High noon. White sun flashes on the Michigan Avenue asphalt. Drum of hooves and whirr of motors. Women trapesing along in flimsy clothes catching play of sun-fire to their skin and eyes.

> Inside the playhouse are movies from under the sea. From the heat of pavements and the dust of sidewalks passers-by go in a breath to be witness of large cool sponges, large cool fishes, large cool valleys and ridges of coral spread silent in the soak of the ocean floor thousands of years.

> A naked swimmer dives. A knife in his right hand shoots a streak at the throat of a shark. The tail of the shark lashes. One swing would kill the swimmer ... Soon the knife goes into the soft underneck of the veering fish ... Its mouthful of teeth, each tooth a dagger itself, set row on row, glistens when the shuddering, yawning cadaver is hauled up by the brothers of the swimmer.

> Outside, in the street is the murmur and singing of life in the sun – horses, motors, women trapesing along in flimsy clothes, play of sunfire in their blood.

Comments

1. **Content and mood:** this is a very physical, sensuous poem, set in a big North American city, Chicago, in a summer heat difficult to imagine within British experience. However, everyone will have felt to some extent the weariness brought on by very hot weather, or by contrast the surge of energy, the freedom of the outdoors when summer arrives. Both those experiences, lassitude and exultation, are contained in the poem, together with contrasting images; the cool of the sea with the hot asphalt, and the savagery of hunting with the (superficial) civilisation of the city. The ironic implication is that the same passionate life and death struggle goes on in both contexts.
2. **Structure and approach:** the sense impressions in note-form predominate, like the dots of colour from an impressionist painter's brush. That is the major poetic form though there are less obvious ones; the echo of the first stanza in the last lines, the repeated phrase 'long cool', and the chains of images which reflect and contrast with each other.
3. **Language:** the language is highly sensory – sound, sight and movement in particular. At this level the vocabulary is simple, but these simple sense observations build up as phrases into chains of unusual images: 'play of sun-fire', 'go in a breath', 'soak of the ocean floor', 'shoots a streak'. This composite, cumulative effect is the secret of the poem's technique.

Possibilities

The poem is a rich source of images, and groups might search for images in the poem, making two lists, the hot and the cool.

The title is intriguing – a riddle. It could be left off the copy given to the class, and they might try to select one for it – either out of the images in the poem, or creating one completely freely.

The technique of sense impression notes is one which is eminently suitable for creative writing (see Chapter 9). The poem could be a model for a parallel based on a local town in summer, or by contrast in winter, with all the images reversed.

Many of the words have American associations. Would English equivalents have the same force? Could the setting be transcribed to an English scene successfully?

Although the images are strong in the medium of the written word, they could be explored in a different medium by reference to photographs or film; cities at a time when horses still shared the streets with cars or underwater scenes of the sea-bed or shark-fishing. Pupils might enjoy looking through resource books or magazines such as the *National Geographic* for the right pictures to illustrate the poem.

Searching for illustrations leads on to producing a tape/slide programme. The chosen illustrations would be photographed using transparency film and put into a suitable order to accompany a reading of the poem recorded on a cassette tape.

Media Studies work might focus on image chains. Many television advertisements work by flashing a succession of quick-fire images onto the screen to build up associations around a product. After analysing suitable adverts, use a simple video camera and recorder to build up a quick fire succession of images on say 'our school' or 'playtime' or 'energy' – even 'boredom'.

Appendix 1b: Poetry workshops

The Grub Street suite

The following section is made up of six simulations, written as assignment worksheets to be issued to pupils. It is intended that the pupils should work co-operatively in pairs or small groups, since such co-operation promotes and supports the involvement in problem-solving which is central to this approach. The worksheets are written in the format of business memos so as to catch attention – by being unusual, humorous and bluntly down-to-earth. They will, however, need further explanation if that format is too cryptic or if this kind of work is outside the experience of the class.

At the outset, the simulation structure will need to be explained. In all the assignments it is intended that the class should take on the role of employees working in a Grub Street enterprise, undertaking for a supposed client a poetry-related task. Indirectly this practical activity requires close interpretation of a text. The simulation structure may be used just as a springboard to get started, or it could be fully realised, with individuals or groups taking on different parts of the commission and finally delivering a portfolio to the supposed client.

The teacher can take on the role of the client in each case, explaining, amending or adding as necessary. Alternatively it might be preferable to take on the role of the Managing Director who issues the memo or of a department manager within the supposed hierarchy of the business. A third alternative would be to stand outside the simulation altogether, though this would lose some of the fun and motivation which are the advantages of simulation.

Each assignment here is linked to an appropriate text or texts, but it would be possible to substitute alternatives as necessary, with minor changes to the wording of the worksheet. The assignments are not just one-off lessons; they are based on active comprehension techniques which are repeatable time and again. If a class enjoys an activity, you will be able to repeat it by substituting new poems for those given here.

Specific detailed guidelines follow each assignment.

1. Dial-a-poem plc

Memo from the Managing Director

You'll never believe this, but the computer has gone on the blink again and wrecked some of the material we were working on. We'll just have to sort it out by hand again, and I want you to drop everything else in your busy lives and make this a priority. Attached you will find a batch of poems to be unscrambled.

1. In these first two the damage is not so bad. The computer has just lost the line endings and run it all together like prose. See if you can put the poem shape back. Use a diagonal line (/) to show the line ending if you want to save time; if not, write it out in full.

2. In the second one we've only got left the notes that a certain 'dark lady' gave to the poet, one William Shakespeare, when she commissioned the work. If you know it, maybe you can write out as much of the original as you can remember. Otherwise we'll have to send someone off to the library to look it up.

3. The third one is a real mess since the finished poem has been completely wiped out. All we've got left is the poet's notebook, and that's only got the gist of what the poem was about. Again if you can remember any of it, jot it down, but I think you'll have to write your own version. We have a bonus scheme for creativity!

*   *   *

1. The ring and rim of tidal sleep will slip and creep along my limbs and I shall watch, but never catch the final change, the water-plunge, and through what caves beneath what waves I then shall go I shall not know for I shall come from that lost land half-blind, half-dumb, with, in my hand, a fish's head, a shell, a shred of seaweed and some grains of sand.

2. Can I say you are like a day in summer? You are more beautiful and more mild. Wild winds can toss the sweet blossom of spring, and summer lasts all too short a time. Sometimes the sun is too hot, and often there are clouds. In time all lovely things become less lovely by accident or in the natural course of things. But your beauty is for all time and you will not lose it; nor will you ever die when in this poem you live on; for as long as there are people to read this, then this poem lives on and so do you.

3. Went for a walk, very early one winter morning – saw a falcon hovering. Wonderful sight – mastery of the element.

Strong wind blowing but bird swept back and forth on quivering (wimpling?) wings. Sweeping across the sky as smoothly as a skater. I could only watch in wonder. Later before my fire I saw it again and it reminded me of Christ crucified, Christ the creator of all natural things. Then of how we must harness the natural to his purpose. Our drab lives can conceal inner light, just like the embers of the fire.

*

The originals are:

Sleep

The ring and rim
Of tidal sleep
Will slip and creep
Along my limbs

And I shall watch,
But never catch
The final change,
The water-plunge,

And through what caves
Beneath what waves
I then shall go
I shall not know

For I shall come
From that lost land
Half-blind, half-dumb,
With, in my hand,

A fish's head,
A shell, a shred
Of seaweed and
Some grains of sand.

A.S.J. Tessimond

Shall I compare thee to a summer's day? –
Thou art more lovely and more temperate:
Rough winds do shake the darling buds of May,
And summer's lease hath all too short a date:
Sometime too hot the eye of heaven shines,
And often is his gold complexion dimm'd:
And every fair from fair sometime declines,
By chance, or nature's changing course untrimm'd;
But thy eternal summer shall not fade,

Nor lose possession of that fair thou ow'st,
Nor shall death brag thou wander'st in his shade,
When in eternal lines to time thou grow'st;
  So long as men can breathe, or eyes can see,
  So long lives this, and this gives life to thee.

William Shakespeare

The Windhover

To Christ our Lord

I caught this morning morning's minion, kingdom of
    daylight's dauphin, dapple-dawn-drawn Falcon, in his
    riding
Of the rolling level underneath him steady air, and striding
High there, how he rung upon the rein of a wimpling wing
In his ecstasy! then off, off forth on swing,
    As a skate's heel sweeps smooth on a bow-bend: the hurl
    and gliding
    Rebuffed the big wind. My heart in hiding
Stirred for a bird, – the achieve of, the mastery of the thing!

Brute beauty and valour and act, oh, air, pride, plume, here
    Buckle! AND the fire that breaks from thee then, a billion
Times told lovelier, more dangerous, O my chevalier!

    No wonder of it: sheer plod makes plough down sillion
Shine, and blue-bleak embers, ah my dear,
    Fall, gall themselves, and gash gold-vermilion.

Gerard Manley Hopkins

*

The value of the approach lies in the detailed attention given to a poem's structure. Although this worksheet is written as one entity, the three levels of activity become increasingly advanced and are here related to increasingly difficult poems.

Younger pupils should find no difficulty with level one. This asks for a poem which has been written out as prose to be separated out into line lengths again. Further examples could be given, including free verse and concrete poetry to add to the challenge.

The second level asks for a prose translation of a poem to be 'reconstituted' into the original. The most obvious use of the technique is with poems which have been encountered previously and are dimly remembered by the class. Working together they can often recall the whole poem exactly, though that would be out of the question for any one person. The value of the approach lies in the recollection of partly remembered poetry – a revisiting and celebrating of an experience. The example given is a difficult one –

Shakespeare's sonnet no. 18 'Shall I compare thee to a summer's day?' – likely to have been encountered only by advanced classes, but any poem previously encountered by the class may be substituted.

Another important application of this technique is as a means of introducing the meaning of a difficult poem to a class in a comprehensible form *before* they encounter it in the poet's own words, particularly if these are in a less comprehensible form. The teacher writes an accurate prose version of the poem. Although such a process might seem to be blasphemy, pupils later see the poem in its 'true' version.

The third level reduces the amount of information given about a poem to a supposed 'Poet's Notebook' entry. As with level two, the technique can be used either to prompt recall of a poem studied earlier or to introduce the meaning of a difficult poem before introducing the poem itself so as to increase pupil confidence. It can also be used as a stimulus for creative writing, to encourage empathy with the theme or topic of a target poem. The poem is encountered only later, and then through the light of the pupil's own experience of writing. Gerard Manley Hopkins' sonnet *The Windhover* is a particularly difficult poem, used here deliberately so as to emphasise the point. The technique can be applied to the whole range of poetry likely to be found in the secondary school.

---

2. Cloze shop

Memo from the Managing Director

The poet William Blake has had a lot of trouble finding the right adjectives for the poem overleaf, and he has sent us a copy with blanks in it. He would like us to suggest which words might fit in best with the meaning of the poem so far. To give us a start I've jotted down a few words underneath. See which you think would go best.

You should discuss your choices carefully since you will have to convince the rest of us here that what you have in mind is absolutely right for the poem.

William has a complete version of the poem at home and he'll send it along later for us to compare with ours.

* * *

A Poison Tree

I was angry with my friend:
I told my wrath, my wrath did end.
I was angry with my _____
I told it not, my wrath did _____

And I watered it in fears,
Night and morning with my tears;

And I _____ it with smiles,
And with soft deceitful _____

And it grew both day and night,
Till it bore an _____ bright;
And my foe beheld it shine,
And he knew that it was _____

And into my garden stole
When the night had veiled the _____
In the morning glad I see
My foe _____ beneath the treet.

                                 William Blake

enemy	mend	smothered	miles
friend	grow	warmed	files
foe	lessen	covered	piles
mum	come	sunned	tiles
self	stealth		wiles

angel	fine	tree	lying
light	line	sky	prostrate
candle	nine	pole	outstretched
apple	pine	moon	dead
pear	mine	sea	sleeping
			laughing

                      *

'Cloze procedure' is now a widely used reading development technique, involving the deletion of words in a text, the reader then being asked to deduce what word is likely best to fit the gap in the text, using contextual clues. In the original design of the technique, deletions do not begin until the third paragraph, so that the reader has a chance to appreciate the flavour of the text. Deletions are then made every seventh word to give a high level of difficulty, or every ninth or eleventh word for easier variations.

   Applied to poetry, the value of the technique is to get pairs and groups of pupils talking about the creative possibilities of language as they grapple with the text and compare the likely effect of the words they suggest. Other applications are possible, for other effects. A general principle worth following is to delete some elements of a pattern which you wish pupils to notice. For instance, adjectives related to colour, or verbs describing vigorous movement, or words in a chain of images, or onomatopoeic words. In the example of William Blake's *A Poison Tree* given here, several rhymes are deleted from a regular rhyme pattern. Since the other deletions are less predictable, the pupil is helped by a list of 'possible' words at the bottom of the sheet. This is of course optional, and there are alternative approaches – for instance to include some but not all of the 'answers' in the list.

Because cloze procedure was originally designed as a test of reading comprehension, pupil answers are intended to be marked against a notion of right and wrong, to give a score of ability. This is not the best approach when the technique is applied to poetry. As they discuss possible meanings, pupils can often come up with perfectly acceptable alternatives which are not 'correct' in the sense that they are not what the poet wrote. Discussion may also raise good reasons for criticising the poet's choice of words. If one of our aims is to encourage critical confidence, cloze procedure is one means of stimulating divergent thinking and a positively critical attitude to the poems studied.

---

3.   Grub Street poetry shop

Memo from the Managing Director

We need more material on cats; it's always a popular subject and we are always being asked to write poems or suggest good quotes, neither of which costs us copyright fees.

The President of the National Association for the Study of Cats has asked us to supply some really vivid quotes for a speech about attitudes towards cats today. What I want you to do is:

1. Think hard about cats for a couple of minutes. Don't speak to anyone else in the team and then you will not be distracted.

2. Try to get a picture in your mind of one particular cat. Close your eyes if it helps (no cat-napping though!). Try to see it doing something, and really catch the quality of its movement with all your senses. Jot down notes of what you see.

3. Call up a contrasting image – another cat, another time/ place/action. Go for colour, texture, the feel of the movement. Compare it with other experiences. Again jot down notes, but still do not talk to anyone else.

4. Look over your notes and try to shape your ideas – just into phrases; don't try to write anything longer. We really need only the most important ideas at this stage.

5. Now talk with the rest of the team about your experiences; then share your writing with them. Listen carefully to what everyone else has written. Pick out the most vivid phrases; suggest changes to make the others more vivid.

6. Once you've sorted out your own ideas, browse through anthologies for published poems about cats. Talk them over and compare their images with your own.

7. Write out a list of quotes for the President of the Society for the Study of Cats to use. Be prepared to read them out to the Board of Directors who will make the final selection.

* * *

Our computer data-base gives the following list of suggestions:

Edward Braithwaite   *The Cat*
Alan Brownjohn   *Cat*
Richard Church   *The Cat*
Elizabeth Coatsworth   *Calling in the Cat*
T.S. Eliot   *Old Possum's Book of Practical Cats*
Eleanor Farjeon   *Cats sleep anywhere*
Alexander Gray   *On a Cat Ageing*
Michael Hamburger   *London Tom-Cat*
Ted Hughes   *Esther's Tomcat*
Vachel Lindsay   *The Mysterious Cat*
George Macbeth   *Fourteen Ways of Touching the Peter*
Don Marquis   *The Tom Cat*
Rosalie Moore   *Catalogue*
E.V. Rieu   *The Lost Cat*
Christopher Smart   *My Cat Jeoffrey*
Hal Summers   *My Old Cat*
May Swenson   *Cat and the Weather*
A.S.J. Tessimond   *Cats*

(Sources for these poems may be found in *Where's that Poem?* by Helen Morris (Basil Blackwell, 1984).)

*

This is an example of the 'cluster' technique, whereby a collection of poems with contrasting viewpoints is studied rather than just one or two, thus allowing pupils the scope to find viewpoints with which they identify. There are very many poems available on cats and the accompanying cluster is just a small selection. People's feelings about cats vary widely, and a class usually holds opinions across the whole loving/loathing spectrum. If we are trying to generate a liking for poetry, then it is important that we give pupils the chance to find poems they can identify with. Not everyone will identify with an idealised cat picture.

In this assignment, the technique is linked to a creative writing exercise so that pupils can become involved personally in the subject. Thus they commit themselves to taking a stance before they are confronted by someone else's viewpoint in the form of a poem. The instructions therefore are in sequence, to direct the creative writing activity. The poem cluster could be delayed longer, until after pupils have composed finished poems themselves; but to go so far might close the subject for them, making the task of selecting quotations less meaningful. Selecting suitable quotations is a mechanism for focusing on images within a text and so encouraging individual taste in poetry.

The Board of Directors referred to in the last line of the 'memo' can be formed by the whole class acting in a new role, to comment constructively on the suggestions of the separate groups who report back formally to it.

---

4. Projects unlimited

Memo from the Managing Director

We have been asked by a local school to design for them a project for one class based on the attached poem. They want it to last for a whole term and to include as many different kinds of work as possible: art, music, drama, tape-recording, all kinds of writing, group work. They are not sure which class it would be most suitable for, so you can suggest what you think best.

For the overall plan I think a web chart would give them the best idea. You can colour code it for the different kinds of work, and number the items for the most likely sequence.

After that you will need to include specifications to guide the teacher – for example sketches of collages and art-work, a sample of a playscript, directions for making papier mâché models.

We haven't much time for a polished draft, so go for quick results – a rough idea of how several things might work out rather than one idea in detail.

Present your first rough outline formally to the Board of Directors which meets very soon.

* * *

All the world's a stage,
And all the men and women merely players:
They have their exits and their entrances;
And one man in his time plays many parts,
His acts being seven ages. At first the infant,
Mewling and puking in the nurse's arms.
And then the whining school-boy, with his satchel,
And shining morning face, creeping like snail
Unwillingly to school. And then the lover,
Sighing like furnace, with a woeful ballad
Made to his mistress' eyebrow. Then a soldier,
Full of strange oaths, and bearded like the pard,
Jealous in honour, sudden and quick in quarrel,

Seeking the bubble reputation
Even in the cannon's mouth. And then the justice,
In fair round belly with good capon lin'd,
With eyes severe, and beard of formal cut,
Full of wise saws and modern instances;
And so he plays his part. The sixth age shifts
Into the lean and slipper'd pantaloon,
With spectacles on nose and pouch on side,
His youthful hose well sav'd, a world too wide
For his shrunk shank; and his big manly voice,
Turning again toward childish treble, pipes
And whistles in his sound. Last scene of all,
That ends this strange eventful history,
Is second childishness and mere oblivion,
Sans teeth, sans eyes, sans taste, sans everything.

William Shakespeare
As You Like It (II, vii)

*

This is an open-ended assignment which allows for a wide range of activities with different groups of pupils. It might be possible to liaise with a local primary school interested in the class's ideas, or it could be free-standing. Although it is suggested here that the ideas of groups are taken only to the blueprint stage, if time allowed these ideas could be taken further so that the class realised the project completely.

---

5. Choral readings incorporated

Memo from the Managing Director

As you all know, business is pretty bad; people are just too shy about poetry reading, and even the most exciting poetry is read like a shopping list. Things may be looking up now though. There are some people here today who could do our business a lot of good – get us some worth-while contracts to perform in public. All we have to do is impress them!

What I want your team to do is work up a presentation which will really make them sit up. The attached poem should be a good one for the full treatment.

As long as it is in good taste you can do what you want by way of sound effects, mime, movement. Work together as a team and think in terms of using your voices like musical instruments.

Play around with the order of words if it helps, particularly repeating words or phrases for emphasis. The poet is not here,

so we should get away with it – but bring out the heart of the
meaning he had in mind!

*   *   *

Cats

Cats, no less liquid than their shadows,
  Offer no angles to the wind.
They slip, diminished, neat, through loopholes
  Less than themselves; will not be pinned

To rules or routed for journeys; counter
  Attack with non-resistance; twist
Enticing through the curving fingers
  And leave an angered, empty fist.

They wait, obsequious as darkness,
  Quick to retire, quick to return;
Admit no aim or ethics; flatter
  With reservations; will not learn

To answer to their names; are seldom
  Truly owned till shot and skinned.
Cats, no less liquid than their shadows,
  Offer no angles to the wind.

A.S.J. Tessimond

*

A commentary on choral reading is to be found in Chapter 5. The example
given, A.S.J. Tessimond's *Cats*, is partially worked out in that chapter, and it
may be easier to use that script to demonstrate to the class what is meant
rather than give an abstract set of rules for them to interpret.

The blank form is included to direct their attention to major features of
choral speaking. The intention is that they should explore the meaning of the
target poem through its sound, seeking out its intrinsic music and drama,
making a record of their interpretation on the form. The heading *section of
poem* allows the group to tick the appropriate feature they wish to highlight
in any section or line of the poem. For longer poems this section would need
to be expanded to give more space.

It would be possible to leave the assignment at this stage, as notes for an
imagined reader, without any actual performance taking place. A class
discussion where individuals explain and justify their interpretation is useful
in itself. If groups are actually to perform a reading, they will then find it
necessary to translate the interpretation on the form into a coding system on
the script itself, perhaps using coloured pens to underline or otherwise signify
who says what and how.

Reading voice	Section of poem									
	1	2	3	4	5	6	7	8	9	10
1. *Pitch*: high – normal – low (tense – relaxed)										
2. *Pace*: fast – slow (hectic – turgid)										
3. *Volume*: loud – soft (strident – soothing)										
4. *Rhythm*: regular - interrupted (hypnotic – dramatic)										
5. *Tone*: positive – negative (confiding – aggressive)										
6. *Cadence*: rising – falling (climax – anticlimax) (questioning – declaiming)										
Background **7.** *Live effects*: real or simulated (footsteps, clink of cups, door banging)										
8. *Recorded*: music, animal noises, car engine										
9. *Instruments*: highlight or continuous										
10. *Chorus*: repetition of line, echo word/phrase, murmur										
Orchestration **11.** *Solo voice*: male/female? Quality?										
12. *Pair*: contrastive – supportive										
13. *Group*: antiphonal – amplificatory										
14. *Unison*: crescendo – diminuendo										

6. Film-scripts syndicate

Memo from the Managing Director

BBC 2 have commissioned us to write the script for a film of the poem *In a Breath* by Carl Sandburg (see Appendix 1a). I want your group to take this on and to come up with a first draft of the script for sound and camera. Your working guidelines are:

1. Use the standard form enclosed for your draft, giving us clear instructions on the shots as you see them and a description of what is on the sound track at any time.
2. You may use any sound and visual effects that you wish. For instance, the text of the poem could be shown on screen without being heard on the soundtrack, or you might want it read quietly against a music background.
3. You could give us a word-picture of what the camera is to see, but 'a picture is worth a thousand words', so a sketch of what you see in your mind's eye will have a lot more impact when we go back to them with the draft.
4. The sketches give us a still version of the major changes of viewpoint, and these should be numbered in sequence. We need to know more about the movement in between these 'stills', so use the standard coding:

Close-up	CU	(face or detail)
Fade-in	FI	
Fade-out	FO	
Long shot	LS	(group or scene in total)
Medium close-up	MCU	(face and half body)
Pan	PAN	(swing camera around a scene)
Zoom in/Zoom out	ZI/ZO	

5. Be prepared to argue your case before the selection board. We must have a script which sees to the heart of the poem.

*

The filming technique is described in Chapter 8 including a simpler layout for younger pupils. This simulation of creating a film-script out of a poem calls on pupils to 'see' both the actuality and the imagery of the poem. This projection into the heart of a poem by means of a practical and appealing activity makes it a valuable technique. Because film is a popular medium, the seemingly irrelevant introduction to technical terms for camera movement is worthwhile since students generally seem to have an interest in how films are made.

No.	Visual (Sketch or description)	Camera shot (CU/MCU /LS/PAN /ZOOM)	Sound (FX, dialogue, voice-over)

The blank layout for the script guides the analysis of the poem into three parts; what is seen on the screen frame by frame, the camera movement required to capture that scene, and what is heard as a sound track (perhaps with music or sound effects accompaniment). So, on the left-hand side the script-writers sketch the main features of the text as a numbered sequence of frames down the page. In some cases pupils may have built up a barrier to visual interpretation. In our culture as we get older we seem to lose confidence in our ability to draw even the simplest sketches, so it is worthwhile emphasising that pin-men and ground plans without perspective are acceptable. It can be helpful if the teacher is willing to risk personal reputation by giving an example on the board, and here it may be good psychology if the example is not of cameo quality. It is, of course, possible to allow a written, note-form interpretation of the visual – notes for the location manager or camera operator – but this does not ensure that the script-writer has actually seen the text in the mind's eye.

The sound track will most obviously be a reading, line by line, of the text of the poem linked to the visual frames. However the relationship between sound and vision might be more oblique than a line-by-line correspondence.

The visual might at times be a collage with no text heard, or it might change more or less frequently than each line. The technique allows pupils to be creative in their interpretation, and this can make their results refreshingly unpredictable. As for the text, this might be a choral reading, with all the demands of assignment 5. It might have music in the background, and sound effects.

Not all poetry fits the technique, which favours a series of visual images, but the range of possibility is quite wide, including the whole genre of ballads, which have a narrative structure appropriate to the medium.

The process is likely to rest at the production of scripts, since film production is costly and time-consuming, though a powerful learning medium. A much cheaper and more readily available alternative is to use a video camera to explore interpretations, if not through drama indoors or on location, then perhaps through drawings, pictures and photographs – zooming in and out on detail to the accompaniment of a reading of the text.

Appendix 2: A glossary of technical terms

You can walk without knowing that certain bones in your feet are called metatarsals; you can talk without knowing that certain parts of what you say can be labelled theme and rheme; you can be affected by poetry without knowing that parts of it can be tagged dimeter or spondee. You do not have to know a set of labels in order to walk or talk or be moved by poetry. But you might be interested in how it is that we can walk – or communicate – or shape poems. In this case the concepts signified by the labels might be of interest to you.

This glossary sets out some terms applied to various aspects of technique in Western poetry. If they help to make you more alert to what is going on inside poem and reader when the two meet, that is fine. But avoid becoming a technique spotter. Remember that poets meant their poems to be read or heard and felt. Technique is present to help us in that process – a servant, not a master.

Each term is presented in alphabetical order. That should signal that this list is an invitation to browse.

Accent

This refers to the stress on a syllable or word. *Syll*able is a *good* ex*am*ple. You will find that a poem can play with two accents – the stress pattern which its rhythm pattern requires and the stress pattern which the meaning of the poem suggests. That is why it is always a good idea to read a poem out loud, to see how far the two sources of accent match or, sometimes, disagree. That could be a signal that the poet wants you to pay particular attention.

Alliteration

This is also called 'front rhyme'. Many cultures like making poetic language 'special' in some way. In Anglo-Saxon times, the custom was to rhyme words at the front by starting words with the same sounds, a custom you still find in tabloid newspaper headlines. Rhyming words at the end came later.

Here is an Anglo-Saxon hero facing the Vikings:

> Hige sceal Þé heardra, heort Þé cénre
> mod sceal Þé máre, Þé úre maegen lytlað.
>
> Thought shall be the harder, heart the keener,
> courage the greater, as our might grows smaller.

It is rare to find such intensity of alliteration nowadays, but it remains a good technique for getting us to notice and link words.

Alternate rhyme

This is a common rhyme-scheme, in which lines 1 and 3 rhyme with one another and so do lines 2 and 4. Rhyme-schemes can be written in brief. This one would be written *abab*. If you notice that a poem has a rhyme-scheme, ask yourself whether the words which rhyme are being pointed out to you by the poem as important. If they come at the end of lines which stop, they might well be – but look at *Enjambement*, where the poet is playing a different sort of game with you.

Association

Poems rely heavily on association – on suggesting more than they can state. That is partly to do with their compression; it is partly to do with poets wanting to leave you room to co-invent the poem. Allusions, references, analogies, images, metaphors, similes all help you to employ associations. So do the words within a poem as you associate something in line 1 with something in line 3, a phrase in line 7 with an image in line 4, a rhyme in the first part of the poem with an echo of it in the last line.

Assonance

This is a partial rhyme. You could have words which have rhyming vowel sounds but different consonants – 'make' and 'date' or 'heart' and 'park'. You could have words which have rhyming consonant sounds but different vowels – 'store' and 'stare' or 'light' and 'late'. Keats liked this more subtle music in his *Ode to Autumn*. It is a device which can be used to make a poem have some kind of rhyme even when it does not seem to have any, at first sight.

Blank verse

This is verse which has rhythm but dispenses with rhyme. Shakespeare used it extensively, for it was the regular verse form of English dramatic poetry. He wrote mainly in the popular form called *iambic pentameter*. If he suddenly broke into prose or into rhyme, his audience would know that something special was happening – prose, perhaps, to show an uneducated person was speaking; rhyme, perhaps, to show ecstatic love, or to signal that it was time to clear the stage at the end of a 'scene'!

Cadence

This describes the rise and fall of the voice. In poetry, it describes the rhythm signalled by the stressed and unstressed syllables and the clues this provides on how to read the poem.

Caesura

This has to do with cutting. It has come to refer to pauses in a line of verse, usually in the middle. Poets can use this to break the rhythm and bring you up short, to make you aware of some important feature. Look at Tessimond's poem *Cats* (Appendix 1b), where the words are as likely to stop in the middle of a line as a cat is likely to stop without a by-your-leave.

Canto

This term originally referred to the sung section of a poem but it became the label for the extended verses which make up some longer poems. See Lord Byron's *Don Juan*, for example.

Common rhythm

This is the rhythm we usually expect, where stressed and unstressed syllables alternate. If a poet does not use it – or suddenly diverges from it – ask yourself why.

Concrete poetry

Nobody will agree with somebody else's definition of concrete poetry! Poets have long experimented with making poetry more than 'flat' words on a page. George Herbert wrote an Easter poem in the shape of an angel's wings and many comic poets have had great fun writing poems inside the shape of the thing they are writing about. Young children like writing shape poems as well. In books, concrete poetry often experiments with verse shapes, different type faces, linking words and illustrations. It may even aim for surrealist, subversive effects. But concrete poetry can also be three-dimensional, escaping from books in a marriage of words and sculpture. You could create a concrete poem by hanging six heavy glass letters vertically on a nylon cord so that they spun slowly in the wind – so that others would realise, as the concrete poem moved, that the letters were what they said – S P I R A L .

Connotation

The cool, unambiguous definition of a word which you will find in a dictionary is to do with its *denotation*. Anything else which is associated with a word or a phrase or an image is to do with its *connotation* – the further layers of significance which the poem may suggest or which we may bring with us. Poets rely heavily on connotations and expect us to use them, with due intelligence.

Couplet

A couplet refers to two lines at a time
Which may have the same rhythm and must have the same rhyme.

Criticism

Criticism refers to exploring a poem and considering what is found and generated in the process.

Dactyl

See *Foot*.

Denotation

See *Connotation*.

Dimeter

This is a line with two iambic feet (see *Foot*). It can be used to create a long thin poem with a nervous energy to it, so it is ideal for parody and satire. Love poems can be written in dimeter, but the lyrical is a little more difficult in this format!

Dissonance

This refers to the use of discordant, harsh sounds, to create a disturbing effect. See *Euphony* as well. Both these techniques rely on our being aware of sounds in poetry and on our expecting certain sounds to be pleasant and others unpleasant. The meanings of the words may also affect whether a certain sound pleases or disturbs us – so we may be finding more than one effect at a time from a word or a phrase.

Double rhyme

This is the less well-known label for what is usually called *feminine rhyme*. When two lines end with a stressed syllable followed by an unstressed one, and both rhyme, you have *double* rhyme. You can see it in the first and third lines of, for example from Swinburne:

> Pale, beyond porch and *portal*,
> Crowned with calm leaves, she stands
> Who gathers all things *mortal*
> With cold immortal hands.

Elision

This refers to leaving out part of a word, usually to make sure that a poem keeps to its regular metre or to provide for a rhyme. In Shakespeare's time, for instance, the *ed* in 'weathered' would have been pronounced like the *ed* in 'edited'. If the poet needed a two syllable word to rhyme with 'herd', then 'weather'd' would have been a legitimate elision.

Ellipsis

Poems are compressed living space for words. A poet is very likely to leave words out to cope with this problem or in order to make a poem even more succinct. A prose example would be the old saying, 'Some men are wise; some otherwise', where the words 'men are' are missing from the second phrase.

Enclosed rhyme

This is almost like a sandwich – *abba* – a useful form in which opening and ending lines are joined through the sound pattern.

End-stopped line

This is a well-behaved line.
It stops at the end every time.
If it does not stop, it may pause;
Then it will go on.
   End-stopped lines are ones where what the eye sees and what the ear hears or the voice says coincide. See *Enjambement* and *Caesura* for two devices which subvert 'expected' lines.

Enjambement

This is where the meaning, punctuation and sound of a poem do not stop at the end of a line but stride on into the next. This is a good device for showing energy or passion, or for signalling that something is happening, if the poem has been full of end-stopped lines so far. You might prefer to call this a *Run-on* line.

Euphony

This refers to pleasing sound. You may find that the sound patterns of a poem are attractive – those of a lullaby, for instance. *Alliteration* tends to be one means of bringing pleasant sounds to the fore.

Even stress

This is the label for words in which two syllables have equal stress – '*Man-kind*', 'Mid-day', '*Un*-der-*took*', '*Thun*-der-*struck*'.

Eye rhyme

This is sometimes known as *near rhyme*. These are terms for words whose looks and sounds part company: 'bead' and 'head', or Emily Bronte's 'Ladybird! Ladybird! fly away *home*, / Night is approaching, and sunset is *come*'. When a poet is deliberately treating your visual attention in one way and your listening attention in another, it could be worth asking yourself why.

Feminine rhyme

This is an unfortunate sexist term. See *Double rhyme* instead.

Foot

The novelist John Fowles says that poetry started with dancing, not mere song. In other words, it is to do with ordered energy and muscularity as much as with sound. That may explain why the term *foot* remains operative. In English poetry, it generally refers to a unit in *Scansion* which has one strong stress or *Accent*.

Here is a brief list.

Amphibrach	im*men*sely	re*vi*sion	˘ ´ ˘
Anapaest	lemon*ade*	in a *dream*	˘ ˘ ´
Dactyl	*trem*ulous	*wan*dering	´ ˘ ˘
Iambus	des*pair*	cre*ate*	˘ ´
Spondee	*I am*		´ ´
Trochee	*high*ly	*fear*some	´ ˘

There is no point in sorting out what sorts of feet are being used in a poem unless you want to say what sort of dance they are creating – what movements, what mood, what special appeal. Iambic feet are the basis of most English verse and hence the most unremarkable. Lots of spondees or dactyls might result in an unexpected rhythm – dactyls might be handy for a nursery rhyme about going 'bumpety-bumpety-bump', for example. A line of spondees might make for slowness, dignity or melancholy, and it is no accident that the word comes from the solemn hymns sung at certain Ancient Greek ceremonies. Keep an ear open for what a poem's feet are doing; notice where they change and consider why. Notice, also, where you want to read the rhythms differently. Robert Frost's poetry, for instance, often wants you to be aware of regular rhythms and wants you to be aware of the rhythms and cadences of your own natural speech as well. See *Pattern*.

Free verse

This is poetry which has no regular rhyme or rhythm. It is likely to rely on other devices to give it form – perhaps a distinctive layout or, more frequently, a reliance on a theme and on images to hold it together.

Haiku

The Japanese *haiku* is a three line poem, the first line having five syllables, the second seven and the third five. There is no regular rhythm and the poem does not usually rhyme. It relies on its startling brevity and the suggestions that its images evoke to create a mood and insight for its reader. Like some Japanese painting, its simplicity is the result of great discipline. The things left unsaid can be more important than what is on the page.

Heroic couplet

A couplet in iambic pentameter, originally used to describe heroic and epic deeds.

Iambus

See *Foot*.

Imagery

Poets rely heavily on making images — pictures in words — to appeal to our senses and our experience of life, to make us recreate imaginatively whatever is being described. Imagery is often to do with the visual — but that in its turn is likely to make us associate with it all the other senses of taste and touch and sound and even smell. Imagery gives us a chance to contribute to a poem. At its best, it surprises us and reaffirms our knowledge. Think of Shakespeare seeing himself in old age bereft of his art, like winter trees without song birds — 'bare, ruin'd choirs that shake against the cold'; or Norman MacCaig seeing birds leave trees:

> Trees open their rustling hands
> And toss birds up, a fountain, a fanfare.

Imagination

Coleridge said that this is what the poet has to use — 'a more than usual state of emotion with more than usual order; judgment ever awake and steady self-possession with enthusiasm and feeling profound or vehement'. It is useful to think about that as a set of ground rules for the reader as well.

Internal rhyme

This is sometimes also called *middle rhyme* and refers to a rhyme made between the middle of a line and its end. It can be used facetiously, as in 'The rain in Spain / Falls mainly on the plain', but it can also create a sense of energy in a poem.

Inversion

This involves inverting the usual or expected sequence of words in a sentence. It is not very fashionable to do this, but it was once a means of bringing a reader's attention to a particular point, of making sure that certain words had a strong stress on them – and sometimes, perhaps, simply a means of making lines rhyme.

Lyric

This is poetry which was originally sung to the lyre. Nowadays, it is used in the plural (lyrics) to refer to any words which are written to be sung. It tends to be used in conventional literary studies to refer to any shorter poem which expresses the poet's feelings and thoughts.

Masculine ending

Sexism again. See *Single* rhyme.

Meaning

I.A. Richards suggested that we use four 'points of view' to make meaning:
    sense – we expect to make sense and we expect what we see or hear to make sense.
    feeling – we have feelings, attitudes and associations as well.
    tone – the speaker has an attitude towards her or his audience and adjusts her or his language accordingly – this provides its 'tone' for the listener/reader to pick up and interpret the implied relationship.
    intention – this refers to the conscious or unaware purpose of the communication, which must affect the language in which it is expressed.

Metaphor

This comes from the Greek, 'to carry across'. It is to do with shifting a word or phrase from a familiar context to a new one; a way of making analogies. The comparison can be to do with sense, but the poet will often use a metaphor which links emotions as well. Metaphors are a means of suggesting more than words state – of creating resonances of meaning. Look at *Simile* as well. Metaphors tend to be bolder – they get rid of such phrases as 'is like'. 'The sun was like a coin on fire sinking into the sea' is a bad simile. A metaphor would say 'The coin on fire sank into the sea.' It's still bad, but it is more powerful because it is more direct, less apologetic about what it has to say.

Metre

This comes from the Greek for 'measure' and refers to any regular form of poetic rhythm. See *Foot* for various types of rhythm. See also *Pattern*. You can have dimeter (2 feet), trimeter (3), tetrameter (4), pentameter (5), and so on. Iambic pentameter is the most common form.

Mood

In Old English, 'mod' could mean heart or mind – a sensible bringing together of intellect and feeling. Nowadays, we use it to refer to the general tone of a poem.

Motif

This word comes from the Latin 'to move' – an idea which forms the main driving theme of a poem. The motif may not always be stated. Sometimes you will find it through the poet using a particular set of images. (Titles are worth looking at, as well!)

Ode

This form of poetry comes from the Greek word for 'to sing' – a poem to somebody or some ideal, expressed in an exalted way. An ode is a kind of lyric poem. So are some ballads, elegies and sonnets.

Onomatopoeia

This refers to words being used to suggest sounds. Obvious ones are baby talk, such as 'moo' for a cow's call or 'yap! yap!' for a puppy's attempt at barking – but in Danish the phrase is 'paf! paf!', which goes to show that the link between natural sound and our attempts at recreating them is not definite, but is largely a result of our culture. Nevertheless, poets do exploit sounds – think of such words as 'murmur', with its sound reinforcing its meaning, or the Ancient Mariner's ship breaking out of harbour into the excitement of the open sea in its 'furrow followed free'. No doubt you will have noticed that alliteration creates onomatopoeia here.

Organic form

A poem which grows from the writer instead of being invented just to fit a pre-existing rhyme scheme or verse form.

Pararhyme

Rhyme which almost rhymes. The surrounding consonants rhyme, but the vowels change their sound. Look at the poetry of Wilfred Owen, who often used this to create a strange sadness.

> I am the enemy you killed, my *friend*.
> I knew you in this death: for so you *frowned*
> Yesterday through me as you jabbed and killed ...

Parody

A poem which imitates another closely, in order to mock it.

Pastiche

This has several versions, but the primary one is to produce a work in the style of another artist. Parody is a mocking form of pastiche; but pastiche can be a serious art form. Trying to write a pastiche can be a useful way of seeing if you can get inside a poet's ways of thinking, feeling and writing.

Pathetic fallacy

This refers to our ascribing feelings to things which are not capable of them – willows which weep in sympathy with a sad lover or a sky which is as grey as a poet's mood. Poems have often used elements from the natural world to help create a mood in their poems.

Pattern

A poem's pattern gives it a shape and helps the reader to feel its general movement *and* any variations from it. The pattern is a guideline for us to interpret, not slavishly follow.

Persona

This comes from the Latin for an actor's mask. It is an important but difficult idea to grasp. A poem may be written in the first person, but the *I* is not necessarily the poet. The poet can be expressing views and feelings through this created person.

Poem

From the Greek 'to make', 'to shape'. The Shorter Oxford Dictionary defines a poem as 'a composition of words, expressing facts, thoughts or feelings in poetical form'. You might like to work out your own definition.

Prosody

The study of such technical features as verse forms (ode, sonnet, ballad, etc.), metre, rhythm and rhyme.

Rhyme

Words which have identical sounds. See *Single and Double Rhyme* for examples. See also *Assonance, Eye rhyme* and *Pararhyme*.

Rhythm

Rhythm refers to the ordered pulse of a poem. This can be the result of its metrical structure – and some poems (limericks, for example) deliberately expect you to obey their mechanical rules. At its best, rhythm does not come from a sense of mechanical structure and versification rules. It comes from a sense of what the poem has to do; its rhythms will grow out of the need to express the poet's particular thoughts and feelings. If a poet has chosen to use a metrical scheme – for instance, iambic pentameter in a sonnet – at its best the result is likely to be a subtle interplay between the chosen literary form and the poet's own 'voice', with its particular urgencies and cadences.

Run-on line

See *Enjambement*.

Scansion

This involves looking at a poem's use of metrical feet (see *Foot*). This is a pointless exercise unless you are exploring what effect the stress patterns of the language – their music and muscularity – create for you.

Simile

This is the term for an imaginative comparison, introduced by such words as 'like' and 'as'. See *Metaphor* for another form of imagery.

Single rhyme

A better name for *masculine* rhyme. It refers to words which rhyme on the final stressed syllable.

> Only a man harrowing *clods*
> In a slow silent *walk*
> With an old horse that stumbles and *nods*
> Half asleep as they *stalk*.

Sonnet

A popular lyric verse form using a strict discipline of fourteen lines and iambic pentameter. There are various forms of sonnet. The English or 'Shakespearean' sonnet has three quatrains and a couplet – rhyming *abab cdcd efef gg*. Look at the way a poet can use these 'phases' to develop various ideas or progress from one to another, and use the couplet to clinch a point or produce some kind of twist.

Spondee

See *Foot*. (Those two words make up a spondee, by the way!)

Stanza

Lines of verse clustered together. Usually, the pattern is repeated in following stanzas. See *Verse*.

Stress

The emphasis put on a syllable or a word. In much poetry, we talk of *Metrical* stress, the emphases that the metre calls for – but remember that the meaning of the words may expect you to create a different stress pattern. Don't read a poem mechanically. Read it for the meaning you find and create in the text.

Symbol

A symbol is something in its own right which also stands for or summons up something else in the mind and affections. An obvious example is the rose, a conventional symbol of love. Another is the Cross, a symbol of suffering, sacrifice and redemption in Christian religion. Symbols can be very well-known and obvious; they can also be very personal and difficult to grasp. They are always another means of suggesting more than is stated – a means of creating resonance within poem and reader.

Synecdoche

A figure of speech in which a part stands for the whole – Dylan Thomas, for instance, talks of a *hand* which signed a paper, felling a city.

Theme

This term is often used to describe the central idea of a poem. See *Motif*.

Tone

This refers to the general *mood* of a poem and how the writer has signalled it to the reader.

Transferred epithet

It is surprising how often we transfer adjectives to something when logically they belong to something else. We may say that someone's car swerved drunkenly across the road when the car was perfectly sober and the driver was not; that someone was put in a condemned cell, when it was the person who was condemned, not the building. Poets use transferred epithets to condense and intensify what they want to say. They suggest that matters are being 'said' in a slightly unusual way and that we may need to 'see' them anew as well.

Trochee

See *Foot*.

Verse

This word has several meanings. Basically, it refers to the metrical structure of a poem. It is more frequently used to refer to a cluster of lines, sometimes known as a *stanza*.

Vers libre

See *Free verse*.

Caution: These terms are not essential in order to develop response to poetry. They can help you to respond more deeply if you make sure that *you* use *them*. Do not become so preoccupied with them that they start to use you instead!

Appendix 3: Books and journals

The range of books and journals which deal solely and specifically with poetry and its teaching is limited, but there are many publications which include views and information about poetry and teaching. This is a selection of them.

1. Background

Corcoran, B. and Evans, E. *Readers, Texts, Teachers* (Open University Press, 1987). A readable introduction to literary theorists and researchers into the nature of literary response, using both to suggest appropriate classroom strategies.

Dias, P. *Making Sense of Poetry: Patterns in the Process* (Canadian Council of Teachers of English, 1987). Patrick Dias has carried out research work in Canada and England with adolescent readers of poetry. He suggests that there are four basic strategies which they employ and provides support for his argument that these have implications for the classroom.

Dias, P. and Hayhoe, M. *Developing Response to Poetry* (Open University Press, 1988). An account of the processes adolescents use in reading poetry, with reviews of teaching methods and resources from Australia, Canada, the United Kingdom and the United States.

Griffiths, P. *Literary Theory and English Teaching* (Open University Press, 1987). A clear introduction to the work of contemporary literary theorists with discussion of their implications for good classroom practice.

H.M.I., *Teaching Poetry in the Secondary School* (H.M.S.O., 1987). This is no detached commentary but a quietly committed document, arguing for poetry to be a more frequent element of life in school and beyond, and suggesting that it needs to be shaped sensitively, imaginatively and enthusiastically by teacher and pupil alike.

Rosenblatt, L. *The Reader, The Text, The Poem* (S.Illinois University Press, 1978). A key American text on the nature of reading poetry.

2. Journals

Children's Literature in Education (2 Sunwine Place, Exmouth, Devon). An international journal with a high reputation. Articles on the nature of literary response and on classroom teaching, as well as on authors and, occasionally, poets.

English in Australia (Australian Association for the Teaching of English, P.O. Box 203, Norwood, South Australia, S.A.5067). It may not be possible to subscribe to this lively journal personally, but it could be one to be bought by your local teachers' centre or English adviser. It has many challenging, practical articles, including useful ones from time to time on poetry in the classroom.

English in Education (NATE Office, 49 Broomgrove Road, Sheffield S10 2NA). This is the journal of the National Association for the Teaching of English. It is published once a term and carries high quality articles on all aspects of English, including articles on pupils' response to poems and methods of 'teaching' poetry. Its accompanying newsletter has shrewd reviews of the most recent poetry anthologies. Well worth reading.

The English Journal (1111 Kenyon Road, Urbana, Illinois 61801). This is the journal of NCTE, the American equivalent of NATE. It has an interesting range of briefer articles and also produces 'Notes Plus', a quarterly pamphlet of ideas for the classroom, including some to do with poetry.

The English Magazine. An excellent magazine written by teachers for teachers, with lively, often challenging articles. It frequently looks at poetry and has inventive, practical suggestions to make. The magazine also includes reviews of recent anthologies. Recommended. The magazine is distributed by N.A.T.E. (see Appendix 4 *Addresses*) but you should also be able to find out more about it from the English Centre, Sutherland Street, London SW1.

The English Quarterly (Canadian Council of Teachers of English. Box 3382, Station B, Calgary, Alberta, T2K 4M1). This is the Canadian equivalent of *English in Education*. It has some articles on response and the teaching of poetry. Its companion, *Highway One*, is devoted mainly to classroom ideas.

Poetry Review (Poetry Review Subscription Department, 21 Earls Court Square, London SW5 9DE). Published quarterly. A good means of keeping up to date with mainstream developments in poetry, with extensive reviews and some twenty pages of new poems in every issue.

School Librarian (School Library Association, Victoria House, 29–31 George Street, Oxford OX1 2AY). This remains one of the most thorough and detailed review magazines. While it looks at all sorts of books for the school library, it includes some sections of interest when choosing poetry.

Signal (The Thimble Press, Lockwood, Station Road, South Woodchester, Glos. GL5 5EQ). An independent magazine to do with children's fiction, including occasional articles on poetry.

Use of English (Scottish Academic Press (Journals) Ltd., 33 Montgomery Street, Edinburgh EH7 5JX). This journal has long been a forum on all aspects of English teaching, from the philosophical to the very practical, including many articles on the teaching of poetry. Well worth reading.

The Times Educational Supplement. Not a journal, but it carries reviews and articles on teaching poetry, especially in its quarterly supplements on English.

3.   Teaching

Andrews, R. *Into Poetry: An Approach Through Reading and Writing* (Ward Lock Educational, 1983). A stimulating book, arguing that its main concern is to create in adolescents a sense of what makes poetry distinctive i.e. its form. It provides ten 'units' of ideas for each year of secondary school, but the format is flexible. Recommended.

Benton, M. and Fox, G. *Teaching Literature 9–14* (Oxford University Press, 1985). This is a useful book in its exploration of the bridging years between primary and secondary education. While its theme is the teaching of all fiction, it contains several chapters which focus specifically on poetry. Recommended.

Benton, P. *Pupil, Teacher, Poem* (Hodder and Stoughton, 1986). A brief, clear book, looking at teachers' attitudes towards the teaching of poetry before exploring some useful and justifiable approaches.

Brownjohn, S. *Does it Have to Rhyme?* (Hodder and Stoughton, 1980). This was the first of Sandy Brownjohn's enthusing and practical books on ways of helping pupils appreciate poetry through writing it. This is much more than a book about creative writing, as it challenges and helps pupils to achieve a sense of form in their writing. See also its sequel *What Rhymes With Secret?*, published by Hodder and Stoughton in 1982.

Corbett, P. and Moses, M. *Catapults and Kingfishers: Teaching Poetry in Primary Schools* (Oxford University Press, 1986). This book is interesting for those who wish to look at some of the techniques available to primary school teachers. It draws extensively on list and 'twist' techniques and makes a good basis for teachers to devise further techniques of their own.

Dunn, J., Styles, M. and Warburton, N. *In Tune With Yourself: Children Writing Poetry – a handbook for teachers* (Cambridge University Press, 1987). A practical handbook for primary and middle school teachers, to encourage children to write their own poems.

Harris, R. and McFarlane, P. *A Book To Perform Poems By* (Australian

Association of Teachers of English, 1985). A lively collection of 150 poems and ideas on how to make them come alive through speech or movement. The compilers' *A Book To Write Poems By* is a similar anthology-technique book and also worth obtaining.

Hughes, T. *Poetry in the Making* (Faber, 1979). Ted Hughes wrote about poetry as part of a BBC series. In this book, he shares with secondary school readers something of the process that poetry goes through as it is made – or makes itself. A challenging, encouraging book for older pupils to tackle on their own or for the teacher to use extracts from.

Powell, B. *English Through Poetry Writing* (Heinemann, 1968). Brian Powell's book is useful for working with senior pupils who wish to explore some of the many verse forms which poetry can exploit. Powell explains the ground rules for these and offers advice on how to write within them.

Reid, I. *The Making of Literature* (Australian Association of Teachers of English, 1984). A trenchant, determined and stylish book on literature coming alive in a workshop rather than being paraded in a museum. This is a lively mixture of Ian Reid's theories and his ideas about good practice, many of which have implications for working with poetry.

Stibbs, A. and Newbold, A. *Exploring Texts Through Reading Aloud and Dramatisation* (Ward Lock, 1983). A useful book on promoting fiction through the voice and through drama. Many of its suggestions are relevant to working with poetry.

Tunnicliffe, S. *Poetry Experience* (Methuen, 1985). A carefully argued book, starting with the case for poetry's central role in education before looking at practicalities. The book also has much useful information on addresses and good quality books of poetry for the classroom. Recommended.

Appendix 4: Addresses

This is not an exhaustive list of addresses but it should provide some basic points of contact.

Arts Council of Great Britain, 105 Piccadilly, London W1V 0AU. The regional arts associations are always happy to liaise with schools in order to ensure that schools make the best use of their 'Writers in Schools' scheme. If you want to use this but cannot find the address of your nearest Regional Arts Association, the Arts Council will supply it. Teachers in Scotland should write to The Scottish Arts Council, 19 Charlotte Square, Edinburgh EH2 4QF. Teachers in Wales should write to The Welsh Arts Council at Holst House, 9 Museum Place, Cardiff CF1 3NX. The Arts Council in London holds an excellent library of poetry books. Details of borrowing arrangements are available.

Arvon Foundation, Lumb Bank, Hebden Bridge, W. Yorks and Totleigh Bank, Sheepwash, Reaworthy, Devon. The Arvon Foundation provides week-long residential courses on writing for people over the age of sixteen under the tutelage of recognised authors. That sounds worthy and dull. One of us delivered his daughter to Lumb Bank in her A-level year for a week's writing of poetry. She reckons that it was one of the greatest weeks of her life.

Centre for Children's Books, National Book League, Book House, 45 East Hill, London SW18 2QZ. This is the national information centre for children's books, including books of poetry. Its full range of services and publications is to be found in its invaluable *Children's Books: an Information Guide*.

The Commonwealth Institute, Kensington High Street, London W8 6NQ. It is not always easy to keep up to date with poetry from across the Commonwealth. The Poetry Society should be able to help, but the Commonwealth Institute's educational services should also be able to advise in response to specific requests.

The Library Association, 7 Ridgmount Street, London WC1E 7AE. Useful for its lively Youth Libraries Group.

National Association for the Teaching of English, NATE Office, 49 Broomgrove Road, Sheffield S10 2NA. An essential organisation for anyone interested in teaching English. Its journal often contains important and useful articles on teaching poetry. Check with NATE whether it has a branch near you. Local branches are invaluable means of establishing contacts with enthusiastic teachers and locally based poets. Branch programmes often include lectures, seminars and workshops on poetry.

The Poetry Society, 21 Earls Court Square, London SW5. The Poetry Society provides a range of services, including poetry workshops and its 'Poets in Schools' scheme. This is well worth investigating, since it provides schools with access to poets free of charge, thanks to sponsorship by W.H. Smith. Its National Poetry Secretariat can provide advice on its sponsorship of poetry readings and the Society can give details of some of the increasing number of sponsored poetry-writing competitions.

Publishers' Association, 19 Bedford Square, London WC1B 3HJ. The association can supply addresses of publishers. It also has brief, useful information if you decide to take part in the annual Children's Book Week.

Schools Broadcasting Council for the United Kingdom, The Langham, Portland Place, London W1A 1AA. The Council can supply the annual programme of BBC Radio and Television broadcasts to schools. If you want details of ITV educational programmes, contact your local ITV company. Both BBC and ITV employ regional education officers. It can be worth contacting them about their companies' policies towards broadcasting poetry.

Schools Poetry Association, Twyford School, Winchester SO21 1NW. This organisation focuses on poetry in schools through its *Schools Poetry Review* magazine which enables teachers and others interested in poetry to share experiences and practical ideas. The Association also produces broadsheets of poems and 'footnotes' – new poetry which has been cleared of copyright for photocopying. It is well worth sending a stamped addressed envelope to SPA for latest details of its publications and activities.

Acknowledgements

The authors and publishers would like to thank the following for permission to reproduce poems:

'Sleep' and 'Cats' by A.S.J. Tessimond by permission of Hubert Nicolson and the Whiteknights Press. 'Enemies' from *Collected Poems* by Elizabeth Jennings, published by Macmillan, by permission of David Higham Associates. 'Conquerors' from *The Haunted Garden*, Faber 1947, by Henry Treece, by permission of John Johnson Ltd. 'In a Breath' from *Chicago Poems* by Carl Sandburg, copyright 1916 by Holt, Rinehart and Winston, Inc., renewed 1944 by Carl Sandburg, reprinted by permission of Harcourt Brace Jovanovich Inc. 'In-a Brixtan Markit' © James Berry 1985 is reprinted from *Chain of Days* by James Berry (1985) by permission of Oxford University Press. 'Flight of the Roller Coaster' is reprinted from *Collected Poems* of Raymond Souster by permission of Oberon Press.

And for permission to reproduce extracts from the following poems:

'The Face of the Horse' by N.A. Zabolotsky, translated by D. Weissbort, from *Scrolls*, published by Jonathan Cape Ltd. 'Trapezists' from *The Collected Poems* of Louis MacNeice, and 'The Amulet' from *Under the North Star* by Ted Hughes, by permision of Faber and Faber Ltd. 'The Fish' from *The Complete Poems 1927–1979* by Elizabeth Bishop, copyright © 1979, 1983 by Alice Helen Methfessel, reprinted by permission of Farrar, Strauss and Giroux, Inc. 'Midnight's Wood' from *Time's Delight* by permission of Raymond Wilson. 'The hand that signed the paper ...' from *The Poems* by Dylan Thomas, published by Dent, by permission of David Higham Associates. 'Plucking the Rushes' from *170 Chinese Poems* by Arthur Waley, by permission of Constable Publishers. 'The Hawk' from *The Year of the Whale* by George Mackay Brown, by permission of Chatto and Windus. 'Jazz Fantasia' in *Smoke and Steel*, copyright 1920 by Harcourt Brace Jovanovich, Inc., renewed 1948 by Carl Sandburg, reprinted by permission of the publisher. 'Spacepoem 3' from *Poems of Thirty Years* by Edwin Morgan (1982), reprinted by permission of Carcanet Press Ltd.